Grafted In Again

by

Hannah Nesher

Scripture quotations are taken from the Hebrew-English Bible. Copyright © by Bible Society in Israel 1996 and the Israel Association for the Dissemination of Biblical Writings. The Bible Society in Israel, P.O. Box 44 Jerusalem, 91000 Israel

Scripture quotations taken from the HOLY BIBLE, NEW INTERNATIONAL VERSION. Copyright © 1973, 1978, 1984 by International Bible Society. Used by permission of Zondervan Publishing House.

ISBN# 978-0-9733892-4-1

For speaking engagements please contact Hannah:

> Hannah Nesher, Voice for Israel
> Suite #313- 11007 Jasper Ave.
> Edmonton, Alberta
> T5K 0K6 Canada

www.voiceforisrael.net

Copyright © 2008 by Voice for Israel

All rights reserved under International Copyright Law. Contents and/or cover may not be reproduced in whole or in part in any form without the express written consent of the Publisher.

Cover design by James Vanderwekken - jvnderwe@hotmail.com
Editing: Karen M. Gibson

Publication assistance and
digital printing in Canada by

*Page*Master
PUBLICATION SERVICES INC.
www.pagemaster.ca

DEDICATION

To the God of my fathers, Avraham, Yitzchak and Yaacov,

יהוה

אהיה אשר אהיה

To You whose name says

You will be whoever You will be –

Thanks for being all I have ever needed!

And to Your Son and Messiah Y'shuah

ישוע

For your obedience to the Father

For being led like a lamb to the slaughter

For pouring out your soul unto death

So that I could live!

A Special Thank You

I would like to say *todah rabah* (thanks very much) and publicly acknowledge my debt of gratitude towards all the people who helped with this work.

First of all, to my mother and father who gave me life. Thank you for your courage in training up this daughter of yours through all our ups and downs. Although we may not always agree on theology, your love has remained constant.

To David and Juliet for all their diligent work in putting this book together. Thank you for your encouragment and your steadfast faith in the eternal value of this writing.

To my children, Clayton, Courtney, Shmuel (Timothy), Liat, and Avi-ad, who each supplied material and inspiration for my writing. Thank you for your patience with a mother who writes, for putting up with the crazy times in our family, for loving and forgiving me.

To all our partners in this ministry for your love, prayers and support. May you be fully rewarded by the God of Israel under whose wings you have taken refuge!

To Pat & Elizabeth Dupuis for their help with design .

To Karen Gibson for her excellent editorial help.

To James Vanderwekken for his awesome graphic design work on all the books and DVDs as well as editing help with all our DVDs.

I love and appreciate all of you!

Most of all, to the Holy Spirit (Ruach Hakodesh), for granting me the inspiration, motivation, and words to write.

Todah rabah! (thanks very much)

CONTENTS

Introduction...9

1   **Growing Up Jewish**...11
    Junior Praise and Worship Leader...................................12
    Rebellion Against Rules of Men.......................................13
    We Don't Believe in Jesus..15
    Looking for Love in All the Wrong Places.....................15
    Post-Abortion Syndrome..17

2   **Wandering in the Wilderness**............................19
    Divorce - "Me, My, and Mine"..22
    The New Age Movement..24
    A Taste of Israel...25
    University Years: Jesus is the Way................................26
    One Day My Prince Will Come.....................................27
    Just A Piece of Tissue..29
    Sorry, Wrong Number!..31
    Power of Prayer...31

3   **Salvation**...33
    Don't Kill the Baby!...33
    You Know My Heart...34
    The Mourning After...35
    An Angel in the Toilet...36
    Christian Intensive Care...38

4	**Resurrection**..**40**	
	The Vally of Achor Becomes a Door of Hope..............40	
	I Will Never Leave You...42	
	Letting Go..43	
	Born Again...46	
	Atonement Through the Blood.....................................47	
	A Lesson in Reality..48	
5	**From Christianity to Messianic Judaism**...........**50**	
	Happy Valentine's Day...52	
	Jesus is Jewish...55	
	Hineini (Here I Am)...59	
6	**Wolves Among the Flock**....................................**61**	
7	**Two Are Better Than One**..................................**73**	
8	**Confession And Repentance**..............................**101**	
	Child Sacrifice Defiles the Land.................................102	
	Taking Back the Land...105	
	Beauty Instead of Ashes...106	
	The Mercy Seat...107	
	Yeshua is the Way..109	
	A Special Note to PAS Women..................................114	
	Conclusion - Dayeinu...116	

Postscript..**119**

Grafted in Again

And if they do not persist in unbelief, they will be grafted in, for God is able to graft them in again.

Romans 11:23 (NIV)

Introduction

You may be wondering how I, as one who grew up in a traditional, Orthodox Jewish home, came to be grafted back into my own olive tree; or, as some have asked when I share my testimony, *"*What's a nice Jewish girl like you doing in a church like this?*"* This is a long story, but one that I never tire in telling. It is such a wonderful testimony of the grace and mercy of our God who stoops down to scoop us out of the miry clay in which we have got ourselves most thoroughly stuck.

> **I waited patiently for the LORD; He turned to me and heard my cry. He lifted me out of the slimy pit, out of the mud and mire; he set my feet on a rock and gave me a firm place to stand. He put a new song in my mouth, a song of praise to our God. Many will see and fear and put their trust in the LORD.**
>
> Psalm 40:1-3 (NIV)

How did I come to know my Messiah, *Yeshua* (Jesus)? The Father drew me. I did not choose Him; He chose me.

> **"You did not choose Me, but I chose you and appointed you that you should go and bear fruit, and that your fruit should remain, that whatever you ask the Father in My name He may give you."**
>
> John 15:16 (HEB)

It is my sincere desire that this book will bear much fruit for the Kingdom of God – that it will speak to both Jewish people and non-Jews – those who believe and those who do not - yet.

I commit this writing to God and ask the Father in the name of *Yeshua HaMashiach* (Jesus the Messiah) that this work of my hands would be established in order that many eyes would be opened to see the Truth, the Light, and the Way.

> **Restore to me the joy of Your salvation, And uphold me by Your generous Spirit. Then I will teach transgressors Your ways, And sinners shall be converted to You.**
>
> Psalm 51:12-13 (HEB)

This remains Israel's primary mission – to convert sinners to the one, true God. It is my privilege to participate in helping fulfil this divine purpose for it is not God's will that even one of His children should perish. *Yeshua* (Jesus) said,

> **"For my Father's will is that everyone who looks to the Son and believes in him shall have eternal life, and I will raise him up at the last day."**
>
> John 6:40 (NIV)

CHAPTER ONE

Growing Up Jewish

...Christ Jesus came into the world to save sinners – of whom I am the worst.

1 Timothy 1:15 (NIV)

I grew up in a home that was fairly Orthodox according to my Canadian hometown's standards, however not religious enough for the 'real Orthodox' like in New York who wear the black hats and coats and grow their sideburns into long earlocks called *peyot*. My parents kept *kosher*, the rabbinical dietary laws. We used three sets of dishes, cutlery, pots and pans, dish rags and even drain boards. One set was for dairy foods, the second for meat, and the third full set for Passover. God forbid that a non-Jewish person would unknowingly put the meat cutlery away in the milk drawer, or ask for milk with their coffee after a meat meal, since observant Jews never mix dairy and meat products. As a young girl, I never questioned why we observed all those rules. I thought everyone lived that way, as practically everyone I knew was Jewish. I went to Talmud Torah Elementary School, a Hebrew immersion programme. There I learned the Hebrew language, the history of Israel and the Jewish people. I learned about Jewish holidays and customs, the proper prayers for each occasion, and the traditions of my people. We studied *Torah* as one of our subjects, so I knew many of the Old Testament Bible stories: Noah, Abraham, David and Goliath, Samson and Delilah, Samuel and Saul. However, I never really learned the deeper spiritual principles such as: sin, salvation, atonement, blood, and sacrifice. When I drew pictures as a little girl, God always appeared simply as a triangle in the sky – interesting! I was completely bored by synagogue services *(shule)* and at twelve years old after my *Bat Mitzvah* (the coming of age ceremony for a Jewish female child), I declared my independence. I told my parents that they could no longer force me to go to *shule* and that I was now and forevermore staying home to watch Saturday morning cartoons!

Junior Praise and Worship Leader

Actually, when I was younger, I had enjoyed what was called Junior Congregation, a Saturday morning *Shabbat* service specifically for the *Talmud Torah* students. I was often the *chazzanit*, which is the female form of *chazzan*, or cantor, who leads the singing of prayers. In other words, even at an early age, I was the praise and worship leader of the congregation! Little did I know that thirty odd years later, I would be singing praise and worship in Christian churches! From *Talmud Torah*, which ended at the elementary level, I transferred into the wider, largely Gentile world of public Junior High School. Here, I encountered alcohol, partying, teenage boys, and my first taste of anti-Semitism. I had been so sheltered, I did not know that there were people who did not like Jewish people. When I found this out, I did not want to be known as a Jew. I did not want to be different. As a teenager, I wanted to be loved and accepted by my peers, so I hated and denied who I was. I turned my back on my heritage, my family, and my God. With the critical gaze of an adolescent, I could see only hypocrisy and a shallow level of faith in some Jewish people and in the synagogue. My parents forbade me to date any non-Jewish boys. Since prospects for Jewish dates in a non-Jewish school were almost non-existent, and since I now wanted to date like the other girls, I learned the art of deception. Somehow, I came to believe that dating a Catholic was even more rebellious than dating a Protestant, so of course, all my boyfriends just happened to be Catholic, much to my parents' displeasure. My father would, in his anger, warn me, "If another Hitler came and rounded all of us into cattle cars to take us to the death camps, do you really think your *Goyisha* (Gentile), blond-haired, blue-eyed boyfriend would save you?"

I considered my father completely out of date with the times we lived in, and horribly prejudiced against non-Jews. In school we were learning about racism with regards to the Native people in Canada, and I considered myself the lone defender of equality and multiculturalism in my family. Up until this generation, few in our genealogical lineage had ever intermarried. Marrying a *Goy* (non-Jew) was considered a complete disgrace to the family, since God had warned us, the nation of Israel, not to intermarry with the people around us. At this point, however, I completely rebelled against everything my parents believed in. I was the black sheep of the family and they wondered where they had gone wrong with me. How had they failed so miserably, in their eyes, in bringing up their second daughter in the faith of our forefathers, *Avraham, Yitzchak, and Yaacov* (Abraham, Isaac, and Jacob)?

Rebellion Against Rules of Men

At this time, my eldest sister leaned to the opposite direction, and studied at a religious girls' school in Israel. She returned to Canada and imposed a more strict observance of rabbinical law on the family. Suddenly, we had to tape up the light switches in the house so we could not use electricity on *Shabbat* (the seventh day Sabbath). The stove was covered with a tea towel in order to avoid changing the settings. Even toilet paper was not to be ripped on the Sabbath. I thought the whole thing was *meshuga* (crazy or insane). I resented the changes and thought, "If this is religion, I don't want any part of it." Like the vast majority of Jewish people, I had never read the complete *Tanach* (acronym for *Torah* – the five books of Moses, *Nivi'im* – the Prophets, and *Ktuvim* – the Writings of Psalms, Proverbs and others). Because of this lack of knowledge that I shared with most Jewish people about our own scriptures, I had no idea what the Bible revealed about God or what the prophets spoke about our future. I only saw a man-made concept of religion and God, not the true God of the *Torah* who had never asked His people to carry these heavy burdens of man-made rules on their backs. At that, time, however, I did not really care about religion. I was more interested in important things, like nail polish, parties and boyfriends.

Somehow making it alive and still in one piece out of junior high school, I graduated into the greater sphere of high school. There I had a blond-haired, blue-eyed, boyfriend. Every *Shabbat* (Saturday), instead of going to the synagogue, I would go to his house to eat bacon and indulge in immoral activities. Even on *Yom Kippur* (The Day of Atonement – considered the holiest day of the year), while my precious mother sat thirsty and hungry in the synagogue, not allowing one drop of water or one morsel of food to pass her lips on that day of fasting and prayer, my wayward cousin and I were gorging ourselves at the ice cream parlour. Oye! The *Torah* (law) says:

> **For any person who is not afflicted in soul on that same day would be cut off from his people.**
> Leviticus 23:29 (HEB)

I am sure my parents did not know what had happened to their sweet, quiet, little girl. Needless to say, I no longer enjoyed a good relationship with my family.

We Don't Believe in Jesus

In all those growing up years, the only thing I had ever heard about someone named Jesus was that as Jews, we did not believe in him. I knew that there were Jews and there were Gentiles – us and them. As far as I was concerned, all Gentiles were Christians who believed in Jesus, although some attended church and others did not. The only distinction I was aware of in this wide world of 'Gentiledom' was that of Catholics and Protestants. I vaguely heard that they fought against each other in some far off places, but I had no idea why, nor did I ever give it much consideration. That somehow, this *Goyisha* Jesus character might have anything to do with me, a Jewess, was unthinkable. The thought never crossed my mind.

I am reminded of the day that, as a student teacher, I took my behaviourally disturbed seventh grade class on a field trip to the Japanese Consulate. As part of their presentation, the Japanese representative described life in a junior high school in Japan. She showed the awe-struck students pictures of the Japanese school uniforms. One precocious youngster shot out a question, "What if one of the students refuses to wear a uniform?"

The Japanese representative just stood there dumbstruck for a moment before answering, "That would simply be unthinkable!"

As far as the East is from the West - that is how far removed the thought of the Christian Jesus was from my young Jewish mind.

Looking for Love in All the Wrong Places

At the age of seventeen, I left home for college in Eastern Canada not only to study Animal Health Technology but also to escape what I considered an oppresive family situation.

Life became increasingly painful as I wandered from one broken relationship to another. Not understanding what the *Torah* had to say about relationships and the sanctity of marriage, I lived according to the prevailing moral standards of my generation and environment which in a college dorm is appalling. I was looking for love in all the wrong places.

Eventually, one love-me-and-leave-me relationship broke my heart, and out of sheer stupidity and probably as a backlash from the sting of rejection, I agreed to marry the first man who asked me. He was ten years older than I, Catholic, divorced, and in dire financial straits. My first act of mercy was to pay his child support so that the authorities would not throw him in jail. Even his alcoholism did not deter me from this hasty marriage. My father used to tell me, "For such a smart girl in school, you have absolutely no common sense!" Unfortunately, that was true. I simply would not listen to wisdom or correction. The Proverbs tell us that only a fool will not listen to correction. I certainly used to fit into that category, and fools suffer the consequences of their careless ways, as did I.

When my parents heard I was marrying a Catholic man, they refused to attend the wedding, although my mother sent a lovely basket of flowers, to show me that her love remained steadfast no matter what I had done.

In all fairness, my husband tried to be a good husband and father, but I was too young and immature, thinking pastures might prove to be greener on the other side of the fence. Two other factors served to destroy our marriage and became highly significant later in my spiritual life. The first was that my husband had been highly involved in psychic phenomena such as séances and such, which led me in the dangerous direction of the occult. The other was that early in our marriage, I developed health complications that required the removal of a kidney. When the doctor found that I was also pregnant, he performed a D&C[1]. Thus, I lost my firstborn, who belongs to God, to abortion.

---

1 Dilation and curretage - a minor surgical procedure to scrape the lining of the uterus.

Post-Abortion Syndrome

Even though it was termed a medical necessity, I still felt defiled. I had never been in a hospital before and the medical staff insensitively put me in a maternity ward. That was over thirty years ago.

When I returned home, I just couldn't seem to recover. I fell into a deep, dark depression. I sat in our empty apartment, disconnected the phone, and refused to answer the door. I completely lost my will to live and any desire for my husband evaporated. I would go to bed at night weeping, asking my husband why I should want to wake up in the morning. He had no answers for me that could bring comfort to my soul.

I later found out that a spirit of death often follows a woman who has submitted her unborn child to abortion. As a spiritual consequence of this grave sin, a recurring death wish may result. The woman, not really understanding why, often suffers from severe depression and feels she would prefer death to life. Only by squarely facing the sin, repenting, and finding forgiveness through the blood of *Yeshua* (Jesus) can a woman be set free from this horrible bondage.

Even though I was not consciously aware of the degree of trauma I had experienced, my spirit grieved the purposeful destruction of the life of my own unborn child. Yet, life continued on – a smile masked my true feelings. It appeared to others that all was well on the outside, but I was languishing on the inside. Only God really knows the secret sorrows of our hearts.

> **"The Spirit of the Lord GOD is upon Me, Because the LORD has anointed Me To preach good tidings to the poor; He has sent Me to heal the brokenhearted, To proclaim liberty to the captives, And the opening of the prison to those who are bound…To comfort all who mourn, To console**

> **those who mourn in Zion, To give them beauty for ashes, The oil of joy for mourning, The garment of praise for the spirit of heaviness…"**
>
> Isaiah 61:1-3 (HEB)

The Messiah *Yeshua* (Jesus), read these very passages in the synagogue on the Sabbath Day, claiming that these scriptures had been fulfilled with His coming (Luke 4:16-21). Only He can truly heal us.

CHAPTER TWO

Wandering in the Wilderness

Holistic Health and New Age

> "You shall not permit a sorceress to live."
> Exodus 22:18 (HEB)

After seven years of marriage, the children and I became deathly ill from an incident of formaldehyde poisoning in a new recreational vehicle while on vacation. The traditional medical establishment seemed to bring no relief. Since the test results were normal, doctor after doctor assumed a diagnosis of hypochondria, and offered no answers. Environmental illness at that point was still in its infancy as a legitimate field in the medical profession.

Soon, my weight dropped to less than one hundred pounds since I was sick after almost everything I ate. My two-year old daughter had stopped growing and was bleeding from her ears. My four-year old son's joints were so swollen he could barely walk.

In my desperation, we moved the family to British Columbia where we had heard a doctor was performing wonders in curing this type of environmental illness. In fact, this doctor's cure seemed close to miraculous. After the first treatment, my children slept peacefully through the night without crying for the first time in months. The pain and sickness eventually disappeared and slowly we returned to relative health. This was the hook, however, that brought me into contact with many alternative healing methods. which can be used to draw the unsuspecting into the whole realm of the New Age movement.

One thing led to another, and soon I was deeply involved in not only the holistic health movement, but also Science of Mind, Tai Chi, Yoga, and Eastern Mysticism. The cultures and religions of the Orient had always fascinated me, and so I studied Taoism, Buddhism, Hinduism; anything but Judaism. To me Judaism was a dead religion based on the rules of men and hypocrisy. Christianity was not an option for me because of my Jewish heritage and my assumption that Jesus was only for the Gentiles of this world. Even a Jewish atheist will usually declare, "I'm born a Jew and I'll die a Jew". It just seemed inconceivable to become a *Goy* (Gentile) when you're a Jew. It's either one or the other. I never once considered that the One that these *Goyim* followed was a Jew Himself.

Having never read the *Torah*, I also did not realize how God warned against all sorcery, divination, fortune telling, channelling, astrology, and consulting with psychics.

> **Let no one be found among you who sacrifices his son or daughter in the fire, who practices divination or sorcery, interprets omens, engages in witchcraft, or casts spells, or who is a medium or spiritist or who consults the dead. Anyone who does these things is detestable to the LORD and because of these detestable practices the LORD your God will drive out those nations before you. You must be blameless before the LORD your God.**
>
> Deuteronomy 18:10-13 (NIV)

Of course, I did not consider myself a sorceress. I attended workshops in white magic, but that all seemed to be for good and not for evil. All that time, I thought I was becoming more spiritual and closer to God and the truth. But this was not the God of my fathers; this was a metaphysical God-force, Higher Power or Mind Consciousness. In reality, I was tapping into the powers of darkness, and becoming more and more confused, since much truth is mixed in with deception. That dangerous path began innocently enough with the nurse at the doctor's office demonstrating the art of muscle testing. It is like a form of no-needle allergy testing where the strength of the arm muscle is tested while holding the suspect substance to see if it weakens or strengthens the muscle. She took it one step further, however, and began to ask questions of the spirit within. Soon, I would not take any action, not even a vitamin pill, without consulting my spirit guide. Since my first husband had been involved in the psychic world as a younger man, the passage into the occult was an easy transition for both of us to make.

I have recently read that the powers of darkness specifically target Jewish people to recruit them into occult activities, since this will more quickly lead to their destruction. Even such things as astrology – reading one's horoscope, seeking psychics, using tarot cards, palm reading, crystals, ouija boards, transcendental meditation, consulting spirit guides, and any number of activities that many people consider recreational may prove to be highly dangerous. I would warn anyone involved in occult activities, even those which seem harmless, or just for fun to immediately stop, repent, and seek forgiveness and cleansing from the defilement and demonic bondage that results from contact with the occult.

Divorce – "Me, My and Mine"

One of the basic tenets of the New Age movement I had been indoctrinated into was that "me, my, and mine" was of primary concern. It is the perfect religion for the selfish, sinful, hedonistic beings that we inherently are. Services are advertised as offering "God without guilt"; but, what God is this? Certainly not the God of Israel, of Abraham, Isaac, and Jacob, my forefathers! Rather than righteousness, justice, and mercy, the ultimate goal of life becomes our own personal happiness. There is no absolute standard of morality as taught in the *Torah*; rather, morality is whatever one considers good for oneself at that moment. Therefore, abortion, fornication, and divorce are not wrong according to New Age philosophies; morality is a question each person must decide for himself or herself. I was taught in Science of Mind that what we think determines our destiny. Therefore, if we could only think the right way, then our lives would conform to our own selfish desires. If something bad happens, then our thinking just needs to be corrected. In this false religious system, no sovereign power exists outside ourselves that may determine our fate. We, ourselves, contain God consciousness and therefore can determine not only our fate, but others as well. This is what the Word of God has to say about this kind of belief:

> **"Because your heart is lifted up, and you say, 'I am a god, I sit in the seat of gods'...Yet you are a man, and not a god, Though you set your heart as the heart of a god...Will you still say before him who slays you, 'I am a god'? But you shall be a man, and not a god, In the hand of him who slays you."**
>
> Ezekiel 28:2, 9 (HEB)

The Bible makes it clear that God is the potter and we are merely the clay. Our lives are in His hands, but our sinful natures do not want to admit this nor submit to His authority and standards.

Since I accepted the belief that my personal happiness was more important than the raising of children in a stable home, I decided that I was not happy in my marriage and suggested a trial separation. My husband agreed and moved back to our former home while the children and I remained where we were.

I had such a deep hunger within me for an intimate, loving connection with someone that immediately after the separation from my husband, I began dating. As is common in post abortion syndrome, I became obsessed with a desire to replace the child I had lost by having another baby. Once I became pregnant, however, the reality of the situation hit me full force, and I searched desperately for a way out.

I since have heard the director of a pro-life ministry explain it as if an animal gets caught in a trap and chews off its own limb in order to get free. I, too, felt trapped.

At this point, I already had two small children and was not yet legally divorced from my first husband. Adoption was not even an option for me to consider. It was the reality of the pregnancy itself that I wanted to erase – to deny the moral failure of my life.

Abortion seemed the easy way out. This escape route was provided through a readily obtainable abortion *gratis* through the public Medicare system. Although a feeling that this might be wrong nagged at me, a feminist friend soon convinced me not to be so ridiculous as to even consider an alternative! With a quick and simple procedure, I could get on with my life. Why would I even think for a moment about continuing on with this foolish pregnancy? After all, "It's not actually a baby, but just some fetal tissue". With the decision made, I was anaesthetized and awoke a short while later. All was finished, and I went home to get on with my life. As it turned out, however, the procedure was not quite so simple. The abortion was incomplete – a piece of the fetus was inadvertently left in my womb, causing a haemorrhage.

I was readmitted to the hospital, lying there on a stretcher for hours, bleeding, and being prodded and probed, until I was finally put under anaesthetic again to finish the job. When I awoke, there was no one to drive me home, and my babysitter complained about having to stay overtime. I felt so lost and alone. I hated my boyfriend, but more than that, I hated myself. I had never dealt with the issues leading to that second unplanned pregnancy and the abortion only drove the roots of unresolved guilt and shame deeper into the core of my being.

Eventually, the separation from the husband of my youth became final and we divorced, even though

> "...the LORD God of Israel says That He hates divorce."
>
> Malachi 2:16 (HEB)

My ex-husband refused to have anything to do with our children, even though I begged, pleaded and threatened. As was the case before we married, he was not a willing supporter of his children. So life as a single parent, even though largely the consequence of my own sins, was very, very tough.

The New Age Movement

Searching for help with my problems, I became deeper and deeper involved in the New Age movement. I developed a close relationship with a woman who initiated me into astrology, channelling, angels, crystals, gnomes, fairies, reincarnation, re-birthing, I-ching, tarot cards, palm reading, consulting with spirits, transcendental meditation, all manners of fortune telling, witchcraft and divination. I am ashamed to admit that I involved my children in fire-walking rituals and New Age retreats. All that was a quest to make some sense out of why my life was the way it was and why I felt so rotten most of the time. It was a journey to find myself, and therefore, I thought, find God.

At one point in my spiritual search, I took a well-known psychological test to determine my vocational aptitude in a career workshop – I was a workshop junkie. The test determined that my personality type comprised less than one percent of the population and that although I might do well as a writer, this type of person must absolutely find his or her mission in life or die a miserable, cynical human being. I knew in my heart that was true, and stepped up my efforts to discover my mission. I read books like, *Do What You Love, the Money Will Follow*, and every self-improvement and positive thinking book I could find. Most advised to think right, visualize, and follow your dream. My mother has a saying, which is a paraphrase of several proverbs. She says, "People plan; and God laughs." This was the case in my life as well.

God keeps track of our wanderings. All the days of our lives are recorded in His book. Even our tears are kept in a bottle in heaven. He created us. He knew us before we were even formed in our mother's womb and it is He who has a wonderful plan and purpose for our lives. However, until we are able to declare, "Not my will but Thine be done," we are setting ourselves up for disappointment.

A Taste of Israel

One event which changed my life forever occurred during a trip to Israel, which my parents graciously provided. In Israel, I had a great time with other Jewish young people, and for the first time in my life I felt like I belonged somewhere; that I was home. As I approached the *Kotel* (Wailing Wall) in Jerusalem, I began to weep, not even understanding what had come over me. I touched the ancient stones, and my tears fell upon the rocks. The Word of God says that even the stones of Jerusalem are dear to the servants of the Lord. Was the Lord weeping for joy that

His unwilling, rebellious, prodigal daughter had come to the temple for a visit with *Abba* or were the tears of sorrow due to our continued estrangement and the pain *Abba* knew His child would endure before surrendering her life into His hands? Without even understanding why, all I wanted to do was scoop up my two children, who were staying with my parents in Canada, and return with them to Israel to live forever. I had found a place where it is not a shame to be a Jew. People proudly wear their *kippah* (head covering) and *Magen David* (Star of David) in this land, not as a badge of humiliation, but of honour. I made a vow to return and sought out the *shaliach* (a liaison between Israel and Canada who encourages *aliyah* – immigration to Israel). However Israel, it seemed, was not so anxious to receive a single parent. We could not find a *kibbutz* (agricultural community) to accept us and I had no vocation to ensure us an income, so I switched to Plan B – obtaining a university degree.

University Years: Jesus is the Way

> "The fear of the LORD is the beginning of wisdom..."
>
> Proverbs 9:10 (NIV)

I decided to get a better education and then try again to move to Israel. I enrolled in Intercultural Education at the University of Alberta as people of other cultures and religions had always fascinated me. While attending the university, I studied more about the Eastern religions, but my questions were never answered to my satisfaction, even though my research papers received top grades. Somehow, the concepts of karma, reincarnation, nothingness, detachment, and other Hindu-Buddhist type concepts did not seem to make complete sense.

One day, a friend of mine, who was also a seeker, invited me to go for coffee. He sat down and told me he had finally found the Truth we had both been looking for – Jesus! I was flabbergasted and offended. I asked him why he believed this nonsense.

He answered, "Jesus told me so".

Well, I laughed right in his face, "So, Jesus told you so, did he?" I wondered how an intelligent person could become so childish. I asserted that I was quite sure the cultist Jim Jones' followers believed he spoke the truth right before they all committed mass suicide. For this he had no quick comeback.

Finally, I became angry and said, "There are many paths to the truth and to God. We each choose our own. How dare you sit there and tell me that there is only one way and you have found it and that it is Jesus!" The fact that there could be one objective truth contradicted everything I had been indoctrinated in New Age to believe. He left, probably feeling quite rejected and upset.

I have since heard that he went on to become a missionary in Poland. I am sure he kept praying for me, and I hope one day to thank him for planting that little seed in my life. It wasn't wasted.

One Day My Prince Will Come

Although that sincere and zealous new Christian obeyed the Lord in telling me about Jesus, I still rejected and refused Him, believing it to be unthinkable for a Jew to have anything to do with the one I considered to be the Christian God.

In the meantime, my personal life was going from bad to worse. I was still trying to fill that terrible void in my life with one relationship after another, never knowing the pure love of my Father in heaven. I was engaged to several men and always found a reason to break it off. With each broken relationship, I became more fractured inside, fearing to try again, and still unwilling to give up hope on love, peace, and happiness; and so, the cycle continued.

Just as a securely fastened band-aid is painfully ripped off flesh the first time, those broken relationships tore deeply into my soul in the beginning. After repeatedly ripping the same band-aid off time and time again, however, very little adhesive remains and one can barely feel the pulling on the skin. So, too, did I become accustomed to the fracturing of relationships that had once been intimate. Since the glue was practically non-existent by this time, I was unable to bond. I was placing my trust in man rather than God, not knowing the scripture:

> **It is better to take refuge in the LORD than to trust in man. It is better to take refuge in the LORD than to trust in princes.**
>
> Psalm 118:8-9 (NIV)

Like *Sleeping Beauty*, I had been bewitched by the powers of darkness and was dying inside. What I needed was the kiss of life from the Prince. I could not stop believing the fairy tale that one day my prince would come. However, instead of turning to the Prince of Peace (Isaiah 9:6), I searched for a human prince who would rescue me from that miserable life of mine. I lived with a musician in a converted garage on the beach. When the Bohemian lifestyle did not suit me, I tried on different ethnic groups – dating a French-Canadian carpenter, an Italian businessman, an Egyptian genetics student, a Chinese teacher, a Métis anthropology student, and a Lebanese hairdresser – anyone, but a nice Jewish boy. Catholic, Buddhist, or Muslim was okay, but I would not date someone from that group (Jewish people) that so many hated.

Just a Piece of Tissue

During my university years, I became pregnant once more, and once again subjected myself to another abortion. We had to rent a car and drive through a snowstorm to the United States, since abortions were becoming difficult to obtain in parts of Canada. All along the way, I wondered if perhaps I was making the wrong decision; if perhaps the snowstorm was a sign to head back; but, I could not bear the thought of being tied by a child to this man that I now despised, and so we persevered.

"This is not a baby, just a piece of tissue. Everything will be all right," he assured me. He had been through this before with a previous girlfriend.

A local anaesthetic seemed to do nothing to numb the excruciating physical agony of the procedure; nor did it drown out the sound of the deadly machine that violently suctioned my infant, my own flesh and blood, out of my body. I vowed that I would die first rather than suffer this horror again.

One scene that stands out in my memory of that terrible and irreversible fragment of my life was the moment when my boyfriend, a Catholic, stood beside my bedside and drew the sign of the cross on my forehead just before the abortion. To this day, I know that *Yeshua* (Jesus) was with me, even in my sin, even in my shame and anguish. In my affliction, He was also afflicted, and I know that He longed, even in that moment to say, "Neither do I condemn you; go and sin no more."

God, being a jealous God (*El Kanah*), was not willing to allow my first love to be lavished upon anyone other than Him. Though I belonged to God (יהוה)[1] through covenant, I did not know it, and so He was determined to deal with me in order to bring me back

---

[1] יהוה are the four Hebrew letters in scripture used to designate the personal name of God. The English equivalent would be YHVH. No J or W sounds exist in Hebrew.

into relationship with Him.

> "...I spread the corner of my garment over you and covered your nakedness. I gave you my solemn oath and entered into a covenant with you, declares the Sovereign LORD, and you became mine."
>
> Ezekiel 16:8 (NIV)

I had committed a grave sin in forsaking my God for a promiscuous lifestyle.

> "But you trusted in your beauty and used your fame to become a prostitute. You lavished your favors on anyone who passed by and your beauty became his...Such things should not happen, nor should they ever occur...you made for yourself male idols and engaged in prostitution with them...And you took your sons and daughters whom you bore to me and sacrificed them as food to the idols. Was your prostitution not enough? You slaughtered my children and sacrificed them to the idols."
>
> Ezekiel 16:15-21 (NIV)

Truly such things should never be! It grieves me, now, to see so many women caught in this same trap – submitting themselves to male idols, even sacrificing the children of their own wombs to the gods of immorality through abortion. This is one reason I share my testimony publicly – so that women and their unborn children may be saved from some of the suffering that I endured because of my rebellion.

Sorry, Wrong Number!

Still, the Lord did not give up on this stubborn, rebellious, lost lamb of the House of Judah for whom He gave His Son's very life. God kept calling me, but I kept telling Him that He had the wrong number.

I survived university through all the ups and downs of my relationship roller coaster and graduated with a Bachelor of Secondary Education in Social Studies and English as a Second Language. I found employment in a large high school in a nearby city, which was the place of residence of my latest entanglement. My new beau, a Jewish doctor from South Africa, was a matter of great pride to my parents. I think they finally thought that their wayward daughter had come home – university graduate (with distinction), engaged to a Jewish doctor. What more could a Jewish mother want? However, all was not well. I had everything I ever wanted; I had reached all the goals I had set for myself but I was desperately empty inside. Soon, that relationship fell apart as well.

Power of Prayer

I know that Christians were praying for me. Our family home was situated next door to the president of the Christian University College of our city. I'll bet that one day I will find out that our family was on their prayer list.

There was also a unique Christian girl who witnessed to me in the high school class I taught. That girl was violently disliked and ostracized by most of the students in the class for her outspokenness about her Christian faith. I asked the students, as part of their course requirements, to keep an ongoing journal. In it, they would record their experiences and reactions to the material we studied and I would respond. Back and forth we passed the journals. That girl, rather than write about herself personally, used the journal to witness to me about her faith in Jesus. She would say things like, "If you don't receive Jesus, you're going to hell!"

I would respond, "You can't actually believe what you're saying, can you?"

She would reply, "You'll believe it too when your pants are on fire!"

I laugh now at how absurd her statements seemed to me, but I commend her for her faithfulness in prayer and her courage to brazenly witness to her high school teacher. Years later, I ran into the same girl in a church, and she was shocked. She hugged me and wept and said, "You have no idea how much I prayed for you."

I hope this is an encouragement to you to continue praying for those around you that God places upon your heart. You may not ever see the fruit of your travail, but God is faithful; our intercessory prayers for our loved ones' salvation are never in vain.

CHAPTER THREE

Salvation

Don't Kill the Baby!

Although everything looked in order on the surface, inside I was leading a life of quiet desperation. I had a secure teaching position, a beautiful home, two lovely children, and financial security, but I was seeking something more. I would sometimes drive around aimlessly in circles, asking God to please let me die, since this life was too painful to bear any longer. During the summer months, I filled in as a combination teacher-tour guide for Japanese University students coming to Canada on a short-term basis.

I have always loved the elegance and polite beauty of the Japanese people and so, when a young Japanese man appeared at my door asking to rent a room with an English-speaking family, I welcomed him with open arms. I know we are told in the Bible to be kind to aliens and strangers because we were strangers in Egypt, but I think I took this *mitzvah* (commandment) a little too far! Despite the language barrier, and our differences in age, race, and culture, we fell in love. One starry night, we prayed to the gods above for a beautiful, healthy child. When the child was conceived, however, his family put tremendous pressure on him to return to Japan, and for me to abort the baby. At first, he resisted the pressure.

He wrote sweet notes that read, *Don't ever think to kill the baby. He is a gift from God to us.* He also wrote, *I will never leave you. It is my duty and honour to support you and the baby for the rest of my life.*

However, because of his own fears and insecurities, coupled with the relentless pressure from his family in Japan, he eventually buckled under. The father of the baby also began to pressure me for an abortion. Right up until the very last month, his family offered to fly me to Japan to abort the baby. They continually asked, "Why, won't you have an abortion, Why won't you have an abortion?"

I could only answer, "God says, "Thou shalt not murder."

One day, as he pleaded with me in the kitchen to have an abortion, I became so incensed that I turned around, wielding a large butcher knife in my hand and screamed, "If you want to kill this baby, than you will have to do it yourself. You are not going to send me to someone else to do your dirty work."

After that incident we were both frightened, so we went together to the Pregnancy Care Centre where they explained to him the development of the fetus and the reality that the fetus is an unborn infant, not just a blob of fetal tissue. When we returned home, he insisted on going out for a few minutes. He returned carrying a parcel. In it was my first maternity outfit. He got down on his knees and spoke in Japanese to my expanded belly, tears streaming down his face. When I asked him what he was saying, he replied, "I'm asking forgiveness of my baby."

You Know My Heart

The pressure from his parents intensified and finally he crumbled. He came home one day with a ticket to Japan. I reacted hysterically, but he assured me that he would go for just a few days and he promised on his very life to return. He knelt before me, took my hands in his, and gazed deeply into my eyes. With his own beautiful black eyes, the same eyes his son now uses to charm the whole world, he softly spoke these words, "You know me; you know my heart; I could never leave you nor abandon you – the woman I love and our child. I will be back, I promise."

At five o'clock the next morning, on my birthday, he left. No tears, no hysterical scenes. I think I had accepted that he would eventually leave us. I sat by the phone waiting for his call that did not come. Finally, I tried to phone him in Japan, but heard only a female, high-pitched, heavily accented voice screaming, "No baby! No baby!" He called a few days later to say that his parents were right and either I have an abortion, or he would never help me in any way, and I would never see him again. I felt so betrayed and abandoned, I actually went into shock.

The Mourning After

Thankfully, I had already made contact with the Pregnancy Care Centre which I did not know was a Christian organization. My counsellor, a woman named Brenda, had shown me a video on post-abortion syndrome, about a woman who was running away from life and after multiple abortions could not maintain a healthy relationship. It was called, *The Mourning After.* I saw myself in that video. Although Brenda knew I was Jewish, she gently gave me a copy of the New Testament, but didn't say a word about Jesus. She just looked at me with real love in her eyes, a love I had not seen before, and said she believed this was a divine appointment.

After hearing, but not believing, the news that the father of my baby was not returning, I went to stay with my parents for a while. I could not function. I wanted to die. Man had become my rock and my foundation and now that faulty foundation was crumbling to pieces. A faithful friend picked me up, drove me to my parents, and sat beside my bed for hours while I wept continually.

While at my parents' home, I read the Psalms out of the little New Testament, specially designed for women in crisis pregnancy. It was filled with bold verses of reassurance of God's presence and forgiveness. It said I was not alone. I was not really interested in the other part – the part for the Gentiles – after all, I'm Jewish! Little did I know, this ministry had set up a prayer chain to pray for the safety of my baby and for my salvation. Those Psalms seemed to comfort me somewhat. I read of the psalmist's pain, betrayal, depression, grief and anger; and yet, he put his trust in God.

> **The cords of death entangled me, the anguish of the grave came upon me; I was overcome by trouble and sorrow. Then I called on the name of the LORD: "O LORD, save me!" The LORD is gracious and righteous; our God is full of compassion. The LORD protects the simplehearted; when I was in great need, he saved me...And in my dismay I said, "All men are liars." How can I repay the LORD for all his goodness to me?**
>
> Psalm 116:3-12 (NIV)

An Angel in the Toilet

Finally, it was time to return home and face life again. The pressure for abortion was incredible from all sides. One night at dinner, I could not take it anymore. I was at a hotel, and a friend half-jokingly said, "Look, there is no way you are having this baby. You cannot have this baby – not physically, not emotionally, not financially. Now if you don't make an appointment at that abortion clinic, I will knock you over the head and drag you down there myself!"

I ran into the ladies' room, closed the door of the cubicle and cried out to God for help.

> **I love the LORD, for he heard my voice; he heard my cry for mercy. Because he turned his ear to me, I will call on him as long as I live.**
>
> Psalm 116:12 (NIV)

God must have heard my cry and whispered to a Christian with ears open to the voice of the Holy Spirit that a little lost lamb was in the ladies' room and she should go help her, quickly! The door opened, and I heard a small voice ask, "Can I help you?"

I poured out my story of abandonment and betrayal and she answered, "Twenty years ago, the same thing happened to me, and today, my son is a strong, handsome, healthy young man on the college football team. I have married a wonderful man and he loves all four of our children."

Then she emphatically stated, "I want to tell you something. You can have this baby!"

This was the first time someone had spoken words of life and of hope to me. She also added softly, "I don't want to push anything on you, but I am a Christian, and I just want to tell you that Jesus loves you, and He will never leave you nor forsake you. Even if everyone in the world has abandoned you, He will never leave you and never forsake you."

I did not know this was taken from a scripture in the Bible, but God knew this was what I needed to hear – that there was someone I could count on who would always stay by my side; who would never leave me, no matter what. I had never heard this before. A lot of kids grow up singing *Jesus Loves Me*, but I had never known this love. I thought that His love was reserved for Christians. Although I understood nothing, right there and then I received the strength and courage, with God's help, to go through with the pregnancy.

The woman asked me to come out and give her a hug. When I turned around, she had mysteriously vanished. To this day, I would like to believe that she was an angel sent to save my life.

Christian Intensive Care

Life continued to be a challenge. Many times I felt very alone and God seemed silent. D-day arrived – the day my boyfriend had promised to return home. That evening would be New Year's Eve, when the rest of the world would be celebrating. Instead, I received a package in the mail. It was a journal with his photo inside, and an inscription, saying that he loved me very much, and if I agreed to have an abortion he would return to marry me. I was distraught, and decided to call the phone number I had noticed in the newspaper and had cut out, placing it for safekeeping in my purse – just in case.

It was a Christian Care Hotline offering support twenty-four hours a day. I spoke to a woman who comforted me and asked if she could arrange for someone to call me back. I agreed and a woman named Sharon faithfully called me back. After talking for some time, and much crying, she asked if I would pray aloud after her. She recited *The Sinner's Prayer* and I repeated it, not having the foggiest notion what I was really saying or getting myself into. Basically, this is a simple prayer of repentence and acceptance of the sacrifice of Jesus as atonement for all my sins. Sharon then prayed for some time in a language that I did not understand, and ended by telling me that right then I was in a kind of spiritual intensive care unit and that Christians were going to fight for me until I could stand on my own. Those people faithfully kept their word to stand by me throughout the ensuing battle and I will be eternally grateful to them for their commitment to me – a re-grafted in olive plant in the family of believers.

That woman not only invited me to church, but also came to my home to direct me and my children to their church for a New Year's Eve party. It was not church as I expected, but a real celebration and a great dramatic presentation with a spiritual application.

I remember the music flooding my heart and tears flowing

while we sang, "My life is in You, Lord. My strength is in You, Lord. My hope is in You, Lord…All of my hope is in You." God was wooing me back to Himself in a very special way. What I remember most was how beautiful the people looked to me, and how their eyes radiated pure love. I also ran into my counsellor from the Pregnancy Care Centre at this church! Do you see how it was all a divine set up? I kept going to the church because of the love of the people. I wanted a real person's arms to hold me; not some vague spiritual power called God. That was where faithful Christians showed me the love of God by functioning as His body. They hugged me, phoned me, wept with me, prayed with me and for me – every single day. They gave me Bibles, instroduced me to praise and worship music, and answered my questions. I had a long way to go to understand about the love and faithfulness of this God who would never leave me nor forsake me. I still do. I will not have made it until I see Him one day, face to face. This is my hope and my confidence, that like Job,

> "I know that my Redeemer lives, and that in the end he will stand upon the earth. And after my skin has been destroyed, yet in my flesh I will see God; I myself will see him with my own eyes – I, and not another. How my heart yearns within me!"
>
> Job 19:25-27 (NIV)

CHAPTER FOUR

Resurrection

The Valley of Achor Becomes a Door of Hope

I often end my testimony at this point, neglecting to tell the rest of the story, which unfortunately leaves people hanging. It's like testifying about the crucifixion, but neglecting to mention the resurrection. I was thrilled to be invited to share my testimony on a Canadian Christian television program called *It's A New Day*. Because of the time limit, we ended at the point of climax – when the Christian woman shared the love of *Yeshua* (Jesus) with me in the hotel ladies' room. During the commercial break, a frantic caller phoned the station to ask what happened, in the end, with the baby and his father! One benefit of writing a book is that I have the liberty and time to tell the whole story.

As you can assume, my focus did not immediately shift from an unhealthy dependency on man to a healthy relationship with God. I continued to be obsessed with somehow bringing my lover back to me. Later, I read this account of an unfaithful wife in Hosea:

> "...she said, 'I will go after my lovers, who give me my food and my water, my wool and my linen, my oil and my drink.' Therefore I will block her path with thornbushes; I will wall her in so that she

> **cannot find her way. She will chase after her lovers but not catch them; she will look for them but not find them..."**
>
> Hosea 2:5-7 (NIV)

I believe that it was God Himself who hardened the baby's father against us so that I would come to acknowledge the God I had forgotten as the source of all that was good in my life.

> **"She has not acknowledged that I was the one who gave her the grain, the new wine and oil...I will punish her for the days she burned incense to the Baals; she decked herself with rings and jewelery, and went after her lovers, but me she forgot."**
>
> Hosea 2:8, 13 (NIV)

The more I pursued my lover, the harder his heart became. After I came to an understanding of heaven and hell through an Easter presentation it was even worse. I would write letters warning him that if he did not repent and come back to take care of us he would burn in hell forever! The Lord, however, was wooing me back to Himself; slowly but surely, He was winning my heart through His love and faithfulness.

> **"Therefore I am now going to allure her; I will lead her into the desert and speak tenderly to her. There I will give her back her vineyards, and will make the Valley of Achor a door of hope. There she will sing as in the days of her youth."**
>
> Hosea 2:14-15 (NIV)

One of my first prayers went something like this, "Dear God, I have nothing to give you, but I would like to sing for you. If you would please give me a voice, I will sing praise to you for the rest of my life."

At the next church service, I read a notice in the bulletin about choir practice. I walked up to the choir leader, a big woman with the voice of an angel, and asked, "May I please come to choir practice?" She was a bit taken aback, but agreed on a trial basis to take on this strange, pregnant woman.

So there I stood, growing as big as a house, high on the platform each Sunday, singing to the Lord as I had sung in the days of my youth as a little Jewish girl in Talmud Torah junior congregation. As I sang, I wept, and the Lord began to heal my heart. We were beginning to develop an intimate relationship with one another.

> **"In that day," declares the LORD, "you will call me 'my husband'...I will betroth you to me forever; I will betroth you in righteousness and justice, in love and compassion, I will betroth you in faithfulness, and you will acknowledge the LORD."**
>
> Hosea 2:16, 19-20 (NIV)

I Will Never Leave You

At times, I would receive visions while worshipping the Lord. After going through a long period of discouragement and loneliness, I felt ready to give up. As I began to sing and worship the Lord one morning, my tears flowed freely, and I began to envision from the Holy Spirit a battlefield. Dead and wounded people were all around me. The sound of gunfire exploded in my ears. I knew I had been hit. As I lay there, I spotted a man calmly walking through the battle raging all around us. He quietly knelt beside me and looked at me with eyes full of love and compassion. "No", I said weakly. "Leave me here. I can't make it. I can't go on any further."

He answered, "I will never leave you." Reaching His arms underneath my body, he gently picked me up and carried me close to His heart out of the heat of the battle.

> **See, the Sovereign LORD comes with power... He tends his flock like a shepherd: He gathers the lambs in his arms and carries them close to his heart; he gently leads those that have young.**
>
> Isaiah 40:10-11 (NIV)

Letting Go

One of the most difficult things I found I had to do was simply let go. The Lord had promised me that if I obeyed Him in continuing the pregnancy, He would always take care of my children and me. To this day, He has kept this promise, although He occasionally still needs to remind me that the grain and wine and oil come from Him, and that He is the one who provides all of my needs and fulfils my desires, not man.

During the pregnancy, I was wasting too much emotional energy on the relationship that needed to be in the Lord's hands, not my own. One day, I took a chance and called Japan. Surprisingly, he answered the phone. I begged and pleaded with him to return, even just for the birth of the baby. I was terrified to give birth alone. I began to cry, saying, "It is winter now in Canada, and what if I fall in the snow and ice and there is no one to pick me up?"

Really, it was pathetic. Embarrassed, he said he needed to get his sleep as he had an important meeting the next day and he hung up. I was devastated. That night in the church service, someone gave a word of prophecy that cut through to my heart. " Someone is hanging on to something too tightly, and God wants you to open your hand and release it to Him." I knew I needed to let go, but I didn't know how.

The Lord knows that inside, we are still children, and that we learn best through stories and pictures, and so the Lord taught me in a parable about letting go. My children and I were out in the yard when all of a sudden we caught sight of a black blur. Mittens, the cat, was speeding by with something in his mouth. It was a bird. Although well fed, Mittens never lost the hunter instinct. We caught him, pried open the jaws of death and rescued the poor, terrified bird. Still alive, we laid it carefully in a little shoe box with bedding, food and water. Throughout the day, we attempted to nurse the bird back to health, but it continued to grow weaker and weaker until finally, to our sorrow, it died. As I looked upon the lifeless body of the bird, the Lord showed me that this represented the relationship that I had tried so desperately to preserve. Although I had done all that I could – letters, phone calls, prayers, even sending him updates on the circumference of my expanding belly and ultrasound results – the relationship was dead to me. I needed to let it go. As we buried the little bird in the raspberry patch in the garden, I symbolically buried the relationship and truly gave it up to the Lord.

I know that many people are hanging onto dead relationships, keeping them tightly squeezed between their fingers, even until they become gnarled with arthritis. I hope and pray that you will also be able to let go and let God. He is well able.

On June 24th, 1993, I gave birth to a beautiful, healthy baby boy at home with the assistance of a wonderful midwife. My ten-year-old daughter was with me at times, applying cold cloths to my forehead. My mother and twelve-year old son arrived on the bus shortly after the birth.

I know now why the enemy tried so hard to end this life before it even began. He is a very special boy. We named him after Timothy, who was a faithful disciple of the Lord, also of mixed race, with a Jewish believer for a mother and a Greek father. In

Hebrew, his name is *Shmuel* (Samuel) and he truly possesses the prophetic gifting. Timothy is a light and a joy who has known the Lord from a very early age. He loves the Lord with all his heart, and the Light of the World shines brightly in and through him.

Timothy's father kept his promise to never return or to help us in any way, but I once received a letter asking me to forgive him. I replied with words similar to those Joseph used to comfort his brothers:

> **"But now, do not therefore be grieved or angry with yourselves...But as for you, you meant evil against me; but God meant it for good...to save many people alive."**
>
> Genesis 45:5, 50:20 (HEB)

More important than knowing my forgiveness, however, is his receiving the forgiveness of God through *Yeshua* (Jesus). I have been able to share my story with many people and know that each time, people pray for Timothy's father's salvation. I ask you, too, the reader of this book, to offer up a prayer for this lost soul named Hiroshi.

I believe that tiny, unborn lives have and will be saved through this testimony of God's amazing grace. What was meant for evil God has truly turned for good to accomplish what is now being done, the saving of many lives.

Several years later at the age of five, Timothy spoke to his Japanese Dad for the very first time in a long distance telephone call. I believe, that the prophecy in Malachi will one day be fulfilled.

> **"And he will turn the hearts of the fathers to their children, and the hearts of the children to their fathers..."**
>
> Malachi 4:6 (HEB)

Born Again

Receiving *Yeshua* (Jesus) as my Savior was a starting point. It was an emotional and spiritual decision, but I still needed to understand what had taken place in my life from an intellectual point of view. I eventually bought my own whole Bible and started to read the scriptures from the beginning. Slowly, very slowly, line upon line and precept upon precept, from reading God's Word and asking questions, I began to understand. After a period of time, I learned that in order to demonstrate the death of my old self, full of sin and filth, and receive the new birth of which *Yeshua* (Jesus) spoke, I needed to be immersed in water and receive the Holy Spirit.

> ...Jesus declared, "I tell you the truth, no one can see the kingdom of God unless he is born again... unless he is born of water and the spirit."
>
> John 3:3-5 (NIV)

I did not connect Baptism with the Jewish *Mikvah* (ritual water immersion). All I knew was that I wanted to be as clean and pure as a newborn babe, and so my children and I were immersed in the cleansing waters of the *mikvah* (Baptism) and become spiritually born again. That night after the service, Mittens, the cat, was up to his old tricks again. This time, we caught him running with my daughter's pet gerbil hanging out of his mouth. We pried open his jaws, releasing the gerbil completely unharmed. Although the cat's sharp teeth should have punctured his skin, we could not find even a scratch. The Lord, in His wonderful story-telling way, showed me that this is what He had done for us. He had rescued us from the jaws of death; saved us from the kingdom of darkness and transferred us into the kingdom of His Son who is the Light of the World.

> **He has delivered us from the power of darkness, and conveyed us into the kingdom of the Son of His love, in whom we have redemption…**
>
> Colossians 1:13-14 (HEB)

Atonement Through the Blood

Even though I had recited *The Sinners Prayer* and was beginning to attend a lively, musical, charismatic evangelical church, I still had no foundation in Biblical principles. I simply could not understand what people were talking about when they said, "Jesus died for me".

When a precious sister in the Lord first read Isaiah chapter 53 to me, I could not comprehend the message. Apparently, this unfortunate, unnamed person died to make atonement for my sins. Sins? What sins? I was not aware that I had sinned. I had done my best, I thought, and despite my faults, tried to be a fairly decent person. And anyway, what is a sin?

I thought, "If this prophecy really is about the one they call Jesus, then it's surely terrible the way He died a cruel, tortured death and I feel sorry for Him; but, I didn't ask Him to, did I?" I had no understanding that it is only blood that makes atonement for our sins. The *Torah* makes it clear:

> **"For the life of the flesh is in the blood, and I have given it to you upon the altar to make atonement for your souls; for it is the blood that makes atonement for the soul."**
>
> Leviticus 17:11 (HEB)

This I did not know, even after observing the Day of Atonement for over thirty years! A little niece of mine was boasting about how long she fasted one year on Yom Kippur, but when my Mom asked her if she understood why she was fasting, like most of us, she had no idea.

This is God's way – a blood sacrifice to atone for sin. Who are we to question God? This is consistent with the faith of the Israelite slaves in Egypt. They applied the blood of the slain lamb to the sides and tops of the doorframes of their houses, according to God's instructions through Moses, so that the destruction (wrath, judgment) of God would pass-over them (Exodus 12:13, 23). John called *Yeshua* (Jesus) the Lamb of God who takes away the sins of the world. By putting our faith and trust in Him, the wrath of God will also pass over us.

A Lesson in Reality

Although I had received the revelation of what *Yeshua* (Jesus) did for me when he sacrificed his life on the cross, the Holy Spirit continually reveals more truth to us as we progress in our walk with God.

Recently, I went through an experience in which the reality of what *Yeshua* (Jesus) actually did for us really hit home. I had the opportunity of spending a day as a spectator observing the proceedings in juvenile court. I was angry with the person responsible for my entire morning being wasted by just sitting there. I could not believe he had been so foolish and rebellious as to commit such a petty, stupid, crime. As I sat and watched, I became increasingly angry with the other juvenile delinquents who came one by one to stand before the judge. Breaking and entering, beating another child into a coma, stealing from their mother; the list of crimes seemed endless. I felt pity for the mother I observed venting her anger at her son who was causing all this trouble for his family. I felt no compassion for these kids. Some of them not more than nine years old chose to defy the law and do what they pleased, despite the consequences. All I wanted to do was shake their skinny bodies until their brains somehow fell into proper order.

Suddenly, something caught my attention. A teenage boy

stood up in front of the judge to face his punishment. However, this time, a woman with long, dark hair, stood up behind him – obviously his mother. Although as pained and grieved as the rest of the parents, she stood there with her son and bore his shame with him instead of shrinking back in her seat. It was then that I began to realize what *Yeshua* (Jesus) had done for me. I was like those pipsqueak delinquents, proud and cocky and ignorant in my sins. Yet, despite the fact that I deserved whatever punishment the judge would mete out, *Yeshua* (Jesus) not only stood with me in front of the judge; He looked at me with eyes of compassion and told me to sit down. He stood alone in front of the judge, even though He had done nothing wrong, nothing to deserve it, and even though He knew full well that the punishment for my crimes would be the death penalty. Who can fathom a love like this?

> **"Greater love has no one than this, than to lay down one's life for his friends."**
>
> John 15:13 (HEB)

> **"For He made Him who knew no sin to be sin for us, that we might become the righteousness of God in Him."**
>
> (2 Corinthians 5:21)

> **"For God so loved the world that He gave His only begotten Son, that whosoever believes in Him should not perish but they shall have everlasting life."**
>
> John 3:16 (HEB)

> **"In this is love, not that we loved God, but that He loved us and sent His Son to be the propitiation for our sins."**
>
> 1 John 4:10 (HEB)

> **We love Him because He first loved us.**
>
> 1 John 4:19 (HEB)

CHAPTER FIVE

From Christianity to Messianic Judaism

Some people ask me about the reaction of my family to my faith in *Yeshua* (Jesus). Of course the reaction varies with the individual, but basically emotions ranged from being perplexed to dismayed to out and out horrified. The stigma against parents whose children become followers of *Yeshua* (Jesus) is intense to say the least. Years ago, I grieved to hear that my own parents had *sat shiva* for me after I came to faith in *Yeshua* (Jesus). This is the traditional Jewish custom of mourning their dead for a period of seven days. During this time the mirrors are covered and the family sits in mourning while others come to comfort and feed the family of the deceased. At first, I felt deep pain over this utter rejection of me as their daughter over my faith, but the Holy Spirit comforted me by bringing these scriptures to my remembrance:

> **When my father and mother forsake me, Then the LORD will take care of me.**
>
> Psalm 27:10 (HEB)

> **Listen, O daughter, Consider and incline your ear;**
> **Forget your own people also, and your father's**
> **house; So the King will greatly desire your beauty;**
> **Because He is your Lord, worship Him.**
>
> Psalm 45:10-11 (HEB)

My emotions then moved from sorrow to joy when I realized that my family had only confirmed what the Word of God says will happen to us when we come to *Yeshua* (Jesus). The person we have been, with all our sins and failures has died and is buried with the Lord; and in Him we will be raised to new life. Therefore we were buried with Him through our *mikvah* (ritual water immersion) into death, that just as the Messiah was raised from the dead by the glory of the Father, even so we also should walk in newness of life (Romans 6:4, author's paraphrase). Truly we become new creations. Hallelujah! Our old self is gone and buried. The new person we are in the Messiah is the one who will live eternally.

> **Therefore if anyone is in Christ, he is a new**
> **creation; old things have passed away; behold, all**
> **things have become new.**
>
> 2 Corinthians 5:17 (HEB)

Yeshua (Jesus) said that to enter the Kingdom of God, we must be born again of water and the Spirit (John 3:3-5). Therefore, rather than remain hurt and bitter about my family's reaction, I chose to see it as confirmation of my spiritual re-birth. I also completely understood from where they were coming. My grandfather, Jacob, had fled the pogroms of Russia and Poland. At the young age of thirteen, he came to Canada alone and never saw his parents again. He made my mother promise to never go back to the 'Old Country' again and instilled in her a fear of standing out from among the crowd. Being recognized could mean death. And so they learned to fit in and never cause waves. Because of the history of Christian anti-Semitism, the persecution of Jewish people that took place in the name of Jesus, most Jewish people, including my family, experience a knee-jerk emotional reaction against even the mention of His name. It is as if they have a Jesus allergy which causes an automatic fight or flight response. To my family and many others in the Jewish community, it seemed as if I had joined rank with the enemy. I had dared to be different, to think for myself and make a clear judgement based on the evidence rather than simply following the ways of tradition or blindly following the rabbinic law. Over the years, however, I believe my family has witnessed not only positive changes in my life, but also the incredible love that God's people in the Church demonstrated towards us.

> **"By this all men will know that you are my disciples, if you love one another."**
> John 13:35 (NIV)

The truth is that when I was first brought into the Church, I was simply desperate for love, compassion, and support during a life crisis. I felt alone, abandoned, and betrayed. The people in this church, through the purity of their sacrificial love, brought healing and stability into my life. In the beginning, it had nothing to do with *Yeshua* (Jesus).

♥ Happy Valentine's Day ♥

I remember, particularly, the evening Valentine's service a couple of months after I had come to faith. I stood there weeping from the moment I entered the church. The pastor spoke about the pure love of the One who would never fail us, and yet a part of me still longed for that human love, even if it had failed me so miserably. My heart still grieved its loss, and tears flowed as if there could be no end to my sorrow. A woman standing in front of me turned around with compassion in her eyes, and said, "I believe that you have been terribly wounded and that this wound is not healed. Would you share with me what is the trouble?"

After I briefly shared with her about my situation, she told me her own. She was married with four children and six months pregnant with her fifth when her husband left her to join a country-rock band. If anyone understood what a woman feels like to be abandoned in a pregnancy, she did. Her husband finally did return after five long years of her praying and raising the children alone, but the marriage eventually dissolved.

I know that it was God who placed this woman right next to me that night in the church. She looked at me straight in the eye and said, "You have only two choices right now. You can close yourself off and grow cold, and hard and bitter; or you can open yourself to the love of God and allow Him to heal your heart."

I knew she was right, and I made the decision to keep my heart open to the Lord, to trust in His Word. The Messiah was sent and anointed by the Spirit of God

> **...to bind up the broken–hearted...to comfort all who mourn...to bestow on them a crown of beauty instead of ashes, the oil of gladness instead of mourning, and a garment of praise instead of a spirit of despair.**
>
> Isaiah 61:1-3 (NIV)

I had seen too many women who had taken the other road, and I certainly didn't want to follow in their footsteps. Bitterness and un-forgiveness is such a deadly poison. It not only destroys all those who allow it to take root in their lives. It defiles everyone around them too.

> **See to it that no one misses the grace of God and that no bitter root grows up to cause trouble and defile many.**
>
> Hebrews 12:15 (NIV)

All of us have reason to be bitter; all of us have a story of disappointment and betrayal to tell. This is why the scriptures tell us that the one who trusts in man and depends on flesh for his or her strength is as if cursed, like a bush in the wastelands. But the one who trusts in the Lord and whose confidence is in him will be like a tree planted by the water – its leaves are always green, it does not worry even in drought and never fails to bear fruit (Jeremiah 17:5-8). People may let us down, but God is always faithful. Too many people continually rehearse and rehash how they have been hurt in the past, never letting it go, not realizing that the only one they are harming by hanging onto the pain is themselves. We must let the Lord carry these burdens for us, that we may be healed. This healing is a process, but God is a wonderful counsellor, as His name is called *Pele Yoetz*.

After the Valentine's service in church, I walked past the room where the members of the congregation would gather to fellowship, and noticed that they had set up a kind of cappuccino café in honour of the romantic occasion. That is the last thing I wanted to face at that point, but I heard something that stopped me dead in my tracks and caused me to enter the room with all its cozy candlelit tables for two. A young man sat on a stool playing a guitar and the singing was most definitely in Hebrew. I listened more closely to the words of the song and heard something that made my heart take a leap – it was a song well known and beloved to me. Translated, it says, "Do not fear; wait until you see how good it will be in the next year." I was dumbfounded. This man did not know me; he of course could not have known that I would walk by at that moment; but, God did. The Shepherd knew, and still knows, exactly where his sheep are wandering. He takes special care with the crippled and lame, and with those who are carrying young.

He tends his flock like a shepherd: He gathers the lambs in his arms and carries them close

to his heart; he gently leads those that have young.
Isaiah 40:11 (NIV)

I asked the man why a nice Christian guy such as himself would be singing Jewish songs in a charismatic church such as this? He replied that he had been friendly with a Jewish fellow in university who had taught him this one song. God used him to send a very personal and specific message of hope and encouragement to me – the only one who would possibly understand the meaning of this song. "Wait and see how good it will be in the future for you, Hannah. I have wonderful plans for you. Don't be afraid. I will take care of you."

I think this is the message of God's heart to each one of us. If we would only give our lives back to Him, the One they have truly belonged to since the beginning of time, God will turn each situation and circumstance to good and we need no longer fear.

Jesus is Jewish?

That same night was a dramatic turning point for me in another way, as well. It was the night I found out that Jesus is Jewish. A woman by the name of Meridel, from a ministry in Jerusalem, came from Israel to the church that evening. She was visiting the sister of a woman in the church who had been praying for me. Meridel found out through her sister that a Jewish girl just became saved – Christian lingo for someone who prays *The Sinner's Prayer* and receives *Yeshua* (Jesus) as Lord. She practically ran over to tell me that just because I had accepted *Yeshua* as my Savior, it did not mean that I had stopped being Jewish. She told me that I should never give up my heritage or deny it to my children.

I was shocked! I did not even know who *Yeshua* was, for goodness sake. Jesus I had heard of, but *Yeshua,* who was he? By that time, I had started to get with the programme – attending church twice on Sunday and once for mid-week bible study, and I thought I had converted to Christianity. Now a woman stood before me and insisted that I was still Jewish. I was well past my teenage years, but nonetheless I experienced a major identity crisis. Was I Jew or Gentile? Should I wear a star of David around my neck or a cross?

When someone gave me David Stern's *Jewish New Testament*, it blew me away. I thought. "How can the New Testament be Jewish? It's for the *Goyim* (Gentiles) – Christians!" It never occurred to me that with the exception of one chapter which was written by a convert, it was Jewish people who wrote the New Testament; nor did I comprehend that the first followers of *Yeshua* (Jesus) were all Jews. I was shocked to read how the original controversy was not, "How can a Jew believe in Jesus?" Instead, it was, "Is it possible for a Gentile to come into faith in the God of Israel through *Yeshua* without first converting to Judaism?" It is the Gentiles who convert to the faith of Abraham, not the Jew who converts to the form of religion called Christianity as we know it today.

I could not believe it! It was as if my mind did a flip-flop and suddenly I perceived my faith in a totally new way. This may be called a paradigm shift. It was as if the veil was lifted off my eyes and I could now see this, *Yeshua HaMashiach* (Jesus the Messiah), as our Jewish Messiah. Just as Joseph's brothers could not recognize him, all dressed up as an Egyptian, so too are most Jewish people unable to recognize *Yeshua* (Jesus) as their Jewish brother and Messiah, he being all dressed up as a blond-haired, blue-eyed Gentile. But one day, He will reveal Himself as their brother and forgive all their sins. Just as Joseph cried out, *"Ani Yosef"* (I am Joseph), *Yeshua* (Jesus) will cry out *"Ani Adonai"* (I am the Lord) and a glorious, tearful reconciliation will take place. God promises through His prophets that the people of Israel will recognize and accept the Messiah when the Lord pours out His Spirit upon them.

> "And I will pour out on the house of David and the inhabitants of Jerusalem a spirit of grace and supplication. They will look on me, the one they have pierced, and they will mourn for him as one mourns for an only child, and grieve bitterly for him as one grieves for a firstborn son."
>
> Zechariah 12:10 (NIV)

In fact, the Word states specifically that the wives will mourn by themselves. The only sect of Judaism that segregates their wives is the Orthodox. Can you imagine what a day that will be when the blindness is pulled off the eyes of the Orthodox Jews as they recognize the One they have pierced?

I read in the New Testament when a Canaanite woman approached *Yeshua* (Jesus) to heal her daughter, He stated His mission on earth as having come only for the lost sheep of the house of Israel (Matthew 15:21-24). I am so grateful that God opened the way for anyone of any race, tongue, tribe, gender, and age to come into covenant with Him through being grafted into the olive tree through *Yeshua* (Jesus). I know that those adopted into the family of God are equally as beloved and treasured as those naturally born into *Abba*'s household. There were times when I would stand on the platform, singing in the choir, and from my position I could see out over the hundreds of people in the congregation. Tears of joy would flow as I witnessed the unity of so many different groups – black, white, Native Indian, Asian – all raising their hands and singing in beautiful harmony their praise and worship to God. I later realized that we, together, were fulfilling the scripture:

> **Therefore I will praise you among the nations, O LORD; I will sing praises to Your name.**
>
> Psalm 18:49 (NIV)

This scripture was fulfilled in an even greater way as I sang praises to God among the nations of the world gathered in Jerusalem to celebrate the Feast of Tabernacles.

I have come to realize, however, after living in Israel for several years and becoming deeply involved in the Messianic Jewish Movement, that although there is nothing wrong with wanting to explore the Jewish roots of our faith, we must keep this in balance. I have seen far too many people who were strong, solid Christians become so enamoured with Judaism and Israel that it becomes almost an idol in their lives. Some end up falling away from their faith and denying the Lord, choosing instead to follow Rabbinic Judaism – some even formally converting. It has been very sad for me to witness this – even in several people that I previously introduced to their Jewish roots.

Our focus must always remain firmly on the rock, the cornerstone, which is *Yeshua* (Jesus). We also must beware of becoming so focused on the externals and superficial rituals that we forget the whole point of the *Torah* is love – to love God and our neighbour. This is what the *Torah* teaches and this is what *Yeshua* (Jesus) affirmed as the two greatest commandments (Mark 12:29-31). I have observed that far too often, those who attempt to keep the *Torah* in a legalistic manner fall into a self-righteous, critical, and judgmental attitude towards those who do not, which is in itself a more serious sin than breaking all the commandments they try so hard to observe. If we keep all the commandments but have not love then we are truly nothing (1 Corinthians 13).

I will always be thankful for the unity and love I can enjoy with Christians – my brothers and sisters in the Lord. I will always owe a debt of gratitude to the people in the church who acted as the midwives in my new birth. They nurtured and fed me when I was just a mewling infant – perhaps a touch cute at times, but completely dependent, demanding, and of no real use to anyone. I was so touched by the light and witness the women in the church were to my parents who had come to visit after the birth of the new baby. Every single evening, around five o'clock, the doorbell would ring and someone would be standing there with dinner in hand. One night was Kentucky Fried Chicken with all the fixings; another night it was lasagne and salad. Once it was an entire steak dinner for everyone in the household. Keep in mind, I barely knew these women but they were determined to shower me with blessings to show me the love of God, who lives in and through them. Did not *Yeshua* (Jesus) command us to demonstrate our allegiance to Him through loving one another?

Hineini (Here I Am)

The Spirit of God then challenged me with another question, "Who will go for Us?" I answered, "*Hineini, Adonai,* (Here I am, Lord), if you can use anything, please use me."

The time came, as I grew and matured in faith, to leave that church and follow God's call. It was difficult to leave, almost as if I wondered if God actually existed outside of that one specific church.

I remember one day, standing outside the church in the pouring rain. The gray skies matched my mood and my tears mingled with the rain; for I had been going through a particularly difficult time. Many in the congregation inside were standing at the altar for prayer, but I just couldn't bring myself to join them. Sometimes it just feels like the heavens are brass and that the crisis line to God is either busy or out of service. Suddenly, before me stood the pastor dressed impeccably as usual in his three-piece Sunday suit. We stood there together quickly becoming drenched.

"Why don't you come in for prayer?", he asked gently.

"Pastor", I confessed, "I just feel that it's no use anymore and I just can't bring myself to stand at the prayer line inside."

Instead of trying to convince and cajole me, he just nodded his head and replied wisely, "Yes, I can certainly understand that.

Why don't we just pray together right here and now?"

So there, in the torrential downpour, looking like two drowned rats, that precious pastor placed his hands on my shoulders and petitioned the Lord on my behalf. I do not remember the exact words of his prayer, but this I do recall. He prophesied that the Lord would take this little Jewish girl, as he affectionately called me, all across the nations to tell of the wondrous things God had done in my life. Before God could use me, however, He had more lessons for me to learn. I first passed through a very dark period of time.

CHAPTER SIX

Wolves Among the Flock

One of the most difficult periods happened, not before I received the Lord, but after. Shortly after I prayed the *The Sinner's Prayer* and was adopted into the church, a gentleman approached me with an invitation to a singles fellowship. He seemed a pleasant, articulate man with a large home, apparently financially well off. He immediately cuddled my baby, played with my other children, jumped on the trampoline, and seemed the ideal family man. He seemed intently interested in Israel and the Jewish people and told me that he supported several Jewish causes. I was impressed.

The gentleman began to pursue us with determination. He took my older son camping, fishing, and hunting; also, they built things out of wood, which of course he loved. My son was at the age when he needed to bond with a father figure. A strong relationship developed. My daughter was also indulged affectionately. All seemed too good to be true. During the time I had been pregnant, someone had maliciously said to me, "Who do you think would ever want you, now – a woman with two older kids and a Japanese baby!" That poisoned barb pierced my heart and left me with doubt that I would ever be loved or wanted by any man again. Coming out of a background of dependency on men and addiction to relationships, the thought of living the rest of my life single was an unimaginable torment. I also harboured secret fears that I would not be able to financially support my children. I looked to a man to meet our needs, not yet sufficiently trusting God to be my provider as well as my Savior.

So when this man from Church began to court me through my children, I was both vindicated and relieved. Soon, however, I began to hear murmuring that all was not *kosher* in paradise. My counselor from the Crisis Pregnancy Centre advised me not to become involved with him until he had tied up the loose ends of his life. Those loose ends turned out to be the fact that he was still legally married, although his wife had apparently left him and taken his children away. I felt sorry for him, not knowing the circumstances of her swift departure to another country.

Knowing that he was not yet legally divorced, and as a new Believer, not sure of what to do about the situation, I called an elder in the church to ask her advice. I explained the situation and when she asked the name of the man involved, she nearly shrieked. When I questioned her reaction, she claimed that she was just surprised. She knew this man very well, and she cautioned me to go slow until he was divorced. Others had a similar knee-jerk reaction, but they also covered up their knowledge of the real reason behind their shock.

I regret that few within the church had the *chutzpah* (a yiddish expression roughly translated as nerve) to speak up. If someone had spoken the truth to me in the beginning, I may have been spared much sorrow and heartache.

Soon, he presented me with a long letter, explaining the circumstances of his separation. Apparently, someone in the church had approached him and warned that if he did not tell me the truth, they would tell me themselves. How I wish they had! In the letter, he wrote that he had been arrested and spent time in prison for the sexual molestation of his adopted daughter. He adamantly protested that these charges were completely false;

that there was no truth in them whatsoever, but that his wife was simply seeking revenge for imagined wrongs he had committed against her. He came to me with crocodile tears, begged me to believe him and to give him a chance.

Meanwhile, week after week, I sat under the powerful preaching of our pastor. He spoke much about forgiveness – that we need to forgive people of their sins or else our heavenly Father will not forgive us. I remember one particular week when I was struggling with these issues, the pastor said, *"Do not uncover the sins that the blood of Jesus has already covered."* Later, when I found out that these charges really were true, the enemy used the words of my pastor to cause me to believe that since all his sins are forgiven by the blood of *Yeshua* (Jesus), I did not need to concern myself about them again. I did not balance this with many other scriptures, such as *you shall know them by their fruit*.

Very quickly, in less than a year, I was taken to a gorgeous restaurant in a beautiful mountain resort, where the gentleman proposed marriage. He bought me beautiful clothes that everyone admired, and a diamond ring, custom designed to represent the twelve tribes of Israel, costing many thousands of dollars. Everything was happening fast. In all honesty, the Spirit of God did speak to me and warn me not to marry that man, even rebuking me for making relationships into idolatry – something I held in higher esteem than God; but, I did not listen. My fears, doubts, and insecurities overruled my good sense and my newfound allegiance to God.

When news of our engagement broke out in the church, there were a few individuals who cautioned me against marrying the man. One, especially, was my beloved choir director, who said she had a dream that she was to warn me. Once again I heard from the pulpit and from my fiancé that God's grace covers all sins and if we do not forgive others' sins, He will not forgive us. I had to learn the hard way that forgiveness and trust are not one and the same. One can forgive a snake, but it would be foolhardy to take the serpent into one's bosom.

I never had real peace about the marriage and tried several times to call it off, or at least postpone it. Once, his ex-wife came into the bank where we were setting up an account and caused an incredible scene. She threw front page newspaper clippings at me about his arrest and imprisonment and said, "Here, have a look at the man you are going to marry!" The daughter that he molested from the age of fourteen to seventeen, my daughter was now twelve years old, actually phoned me to confess the truth about the man she called father.

That man was a master at control and manipulation, using threats, guilt, and tears liberally. He knew exactly which of my buttons to press at the appropriate moment. It was only a few days before the wedding, everything was already set into place, I wanted to forgive and forget, and so the wedding went ahead, with all my family present in the Church. Truly it was a beautiful affair, and I made a vow, like Ruth, that God should deal with me ever so severely if anything but death ever separated the two of us. Many times have I wept in repentance for uttering that promise.

On our honeymoon, I knew I was in deep trouble. Since I was still nursing the baby, he had to come along, and with all the stress of traveling, I came down with a severe case of mastitis – inflammation of the milk ducts. Even though I was weak with fever and in a great deal of pain, he still insisted on my *meeting his needs*. "After all, we're on our honeymoon, aren't we?" he insisted.

I soon found out that he had never dealt with the roots of his sexual sins. His will and lusts of the flesh had never been submitted to the Lordship of the Messiah. He listened to no one but the voice of his own desires, no matter whom it hurt. Self was still on the throne. Yet, each Sunday, he went to church and raised his hands, singing, "Worthy, worthy, is the Lamb of God." As for his sins, he would reply, "That's why I need a Savior!"

Shortly after our marriage, he needed to pick up some items

he had left at the home of his ex-wife who now had returned to the city. An argument broke out; he walked away from her towards the car; she ran after him, shouting and screaming. Suddenly, he turned around and kicked her, a blow from which she sustained pelvic injury. I was shocked. He quickly sped away in the car, saying nothing. The police later charged him with assault.

I quickly found out that it was his way or the highway. I needed to clear each and every decision with him, or else a terrible argument would ensue. As a new Believer, someone fresh out of the ways of the world, I had no concept of submission. He would leave books lying all over the house on wives submitting to their husbands, with pages marked and passages highlighted, especially with regards to the area of sexuality. He would throw scripture verses at me continually about wifely submission. Healthy submission is godly, but that was not. One night with tears of frustration, I ripped those pages out of my Bible, later finding the pieces and penitently taping them carefully back into place.

Arguments began to escalate and I feared violence would break out. The screaming and shouting would often carry on all through the night. I knew this kind of home life was harming the emotional well being of my children, but I seemed powerless to stop it. I spent most of my days in tears, and would often run to the river next to where we lived and cry out my anguish and despair to God. "Where are you, God?" Because of the continual and prolonged stress, my body also began to break down. My joints became so painful that by the end, I had trouble walking.

I have learned since, that relationships that provoke severe, negative emotions in us over a long period of time, may become toxic to our bodies, and can be dangerous to our very lives. I heard one woman say, "I'm going to make this marriage work, even if it kills me!" and it did – she died of cancer shortly thereafter.

I still sang in the choir; it brought comfort to my soul. Sometimes I would sit down after choir practice and weep – I was afraid to go home. We lived in an isolated area on an acreage by the river in a trailer, and I knew that if I cried out for help, no one would hear me. Someone had already drowned at that exact spot; I took it as an omen. What I had thought would be my dream – to live a happily ever after peaceful existence on a piece of land, close to nature, with a wonderful husband and my children – had turned into a nightmare. Several times I tried to get away, running out with my baby in the middle of the night. But he would catch us and force us back; other times, I knew I simply had nowhere else to go.

The abuse (sexual, verbal and emotional) was causing wounds that I knew would be difficult to heal. There were times I locked myself in the closet, screaming at him to leave me alone. I felt used, violated and defiled. No amount of bathing washed away the uncleanness. We went to many Christian counselors together, and to the elders of the Church, who told him that a wife is a precious gift and a person, not an object to use and control; but he simply would not listen to correction or advice. Finally, the situation came to a crisis. One night in the middle of a heated argument, he kicked me down to the floor. As I lay there, stunned, I remember thinking, "This can't be happening to me, maybe to some poor, uneducated woman off the street, but not to me – a CJP (Canadian Jewish Princess)! Not to someone who has been indulged and pampered all her life, a university graduate, a woman who goes to church every Sunday."

My first reaction was to call the Police, which I did. He ran and begged me on his knees not to tell them of the assault. He cried and cried, promised that he would change and warned me that if I told the authorities, he would go to jail for a long time, because of the other charges and convictions against him. I thought of my children who adored him, and once again, the fear of being alone and destitute took control. The Police asked me over and over to just say yes if my husband had assaulted me. I said, "No." This proved to be another serious mistake.

I walked into the church that Sunday, bruised and limping.

A woman took me aside and questioned what had happened to me. When I confessed that my husband had kicked me, she was aghast. She began to weep and insisted that we go to the wife of the Pastor. I had been their baby. They had nurtured me through my pregnancy, prayed for me every day, phoned me, cried with me, discipled and corrected me. Now this...

The Pastor's wife assured me that the Church would handle the situation in a godly way without involving the secular authorities. The way they handled it was simply to talk to him once again. They told him that he was destroying me, but of course this made no impact upon him whatsoever. He continued to go his own way.

Not only was his willfulness destroying his personal life, it also was affecting his business and finances. I soon found out that his apparent wealth was mostly a cover up for his huge debt. People began to show up at our door, demanding thousands of dollars in bills that had not been paid. He owed one brother $30,000 but of course, a brother is not to sue another brother in the courts, and so he got away with that situation. At times, our utilities were shut off because he did not have money to pay the bills. The charitable programme in the church once brought us food, knowing that I had no money. He was furious, wanting to keep up the façade of a wealthy man at all costs. Though his finances were in a mess, he refused to give me any control whatsoever, feeling threatened if I wanted to manage the household finances. He continued to spend big money on himself, on expensive ski trips, and buying additional properties on credit. When a financial consultant advised him to declare bankruptcy, he adamantly refused. That self-made man was never going to give in to defeat. So the smoke screen and life of deceit continued.

Through all of that, I met once a week with a few women for a Bible study. We shared the deep issues of our hearts and those precious sisters knew of my desperate situation. We prayed together each week and comforted one another through the bond of friendship and love.

One day, my counselor from the Crisis Pregnancy Centre said to me, "One day, I think God will give you the strength to leave." That day finally came.

One morning after my husband had gone to work, I sat down and prayed, "God, I want to get out, but I can't do it alone and I have no one to help me. So if you want me to leave, I need you to help me get out."

Immediately after I prayed, the phone rang. It was a woman from the church asking if I would like to go for coffee. I declined her offer, but asked if she would want to come over and help me pack. She agreed. She brought boxes and we began to pack. Next, the Pastor's mother phoned. She said, "I can't stand seeing a woman getting kicked around. I'm coming to help you pack, too." That precious elderly lady came and held the babies; I was also babysitting a friend's child at the time. She hummed hymns and brought a complete peace to a stressful situation.

I had no money to pay for a truck to move my belongings, so I went to the bank machine and found the balance of the account just enough to cover the rental of the truck and driver. He came and began loading my boxes and furniture. I noticed the quick passage of time. It was already five o'clock and my husband was due back from work at any moment. I began to panic. I knew that if he came in and found me leaving, there would be big trouble and a potentially violent situation. The driver of the truck also became nervous and wanted to back out, not wanting to be involved in a domestic dispute.

Once again I prayed. "Oh God, if you want me to get out safely, you need to do something quickly! Please help me." The phone rang. I heard the voice of my husband telling me that he had decided to stay late at work to play a game of golf. In all the time we had been together, I had never known him to play golf. I said that was fine and hung up. We got the last of my things out of the house and stored in a friend's basement before he arrived home, and I sought refuge in a local women's shelter. They took me in along with my children, and gave us food, a bed to sleep in, and a safe haven until we could find a place of our own.

I know God helped me escape from that abusive marriage, which lasted less than a year, but the effects of my disobedience to God in entering into an ungodly alliance affect my life to this day. Even David, whom God forgave for his adultery with Batsheva, suffered the consequences of his sin. Their baby died, and he experienced trouble with his children for the rest of his life. His son, Absalom, actually led a rebellion against his kingdom. Rape, murder, and rebellion afflicted his family until his death. God forgives our sins and even helps to redeem the past and can turn whatever was meant for evil into something good; but, we cannot always escape the consequences of our actions.

> **A man's own folly ruins his life, yet his heart rages against the Lord.**
>
> Proverbs 19:3 (NIV)

This separation and divorce had a terrible impact upon my children. My teenage son went straight into rebellion, drugs and pornography. He turned against me, believing me to be at fault in the matter, cursing me and leaving home at the age of fifteen to live on the streets. My youngest, Timothy, who had come to know my ex-husband as his father from an early age, pined deeply for him and constantly talked about all the wonderful things they did together. Even after we moved to Israel, my ex-husband secretly corresponded with my daughter, trying to turn her against me, and visiting her at boarding school, despite the fact that I warned the school of his background and advised them not to let him into the school.

Spiritually, I had to break all ties and connections to my ex-husband and ask that the blood of *Yeshua* (Jesus) cleanse me from all uncleanness and defilement. Besides using the Word of God and the power of the blood of Yeshua to break any soul ties, I also had to get rid of anything that either belonged to him or that we held in common. These are called contact objects. Spirits of darkness associated with or controlling the person will cling to these objects and can cause further harm. Over a period of time, the physical pain in my joints disappeared; but, if I happened to come into contact with him or anything that belonged to him or us together i.e. clothing, bedding, and so on, I would immediately experience shooting pains again.

Separation or divorce is not something that should be taken lightly. It is a serious, covenantal relationship that is meant to last a lifetime. We know from His Word that God hates divorce (Malachi 2:16). I have not written this chapter to encourage women to leave their husbands, but only to bring balance to the issue of abuse in marriage. I have seen some women and their children suffer in abusive or alcoholic marriages. I know that most godly women sincerely desire to be good, faithful wives, and for the sake of peace will tolerate serious mistreatment. I believe there necessarily comes a point where the abuse is not bringing glory to God. I read a book once on divorce and re-marriage that discusses this issue. In it, it shows how the lepers needed to be removed from the camp of Israel and remain outside the camp until they were declared cleansed by the *cohen* (priest). In the same way, unrepentant spouses in serious sin, whether that be adultery, alcoholism, drug abuse, or family abuse, perhaps need to be put outside the camp until such time that they are cleansed by the blood of *Yeshua* (Jesus) through their repentance. Keeping them in the camp only causes everyone to become infected and contaminated. Indeed, we see this in families where these sins are then carried on down through generations. On the other hand, I know of women who disagree with this viewpoint and believe that even in these situations, separation or divorce is not the answer. I can only relate my own personal experience, certainly not a black and white issue, but one with much grey matter. One needs to seek the wisdom of the Holy Spirit for guidance and Truth. I have found that fervent, heartfelt prayer is tremendously powerful (James 5:16), especially when accompanied by periods of fasting (Mark 9:29). Circumstances that just will not budge often undergo dramatic changes when we humble ourselves before the Lord in fasting and prayer. It is an effective weapon of our warfare in the fight to save our marriages and see changes in people that only happen through the Holy Spirit. As a new believer I did not understand this, nor was I equipped to do battle; but, I have come to see and experience that God can change a man's heart.

I have written about this dark period of my life for two main reasons: one is to warn other women to be very, very, careful before entering into a marital or even a serious dating relationship; not to let the fear of being alone or of financial hardship lead you into a disastrous union. It is a serious mistake to allow others to control or manipulate our lives; this is the demonic spirit of the deceiver that we must resist, and submit instead to God. Our God is merciful and He hears our cries, He does not rejoice over oppression of the weak by the strong. If one is already entangled in an abusive relationship, there is hope; there is a way out. God can provide a way of escape.

My other motive is to speak to those in leadership positions in a church or congregation to be watchful over their flocks, especially protecting the baby lambs from the wolves. The word of God warns us that in the last days, men will be evil and will sneak their way into the lives of weak-willed women, loaded with sins (2 Timothy 3:6). Some of these deceitful men will slip into our congregations. We will know them by their fruit. Our Good Shepherd gave His very life for His sheep as would any true shepherd. Pastors, elders, and leaders of congregations must keep careful watch and take steps to protect those God has given into their care. The church is not for the righteous but for sinners, just as the hospital is not for the healthy but the sick. As such, a house for repentant sinners, it will be necessarily full of problems. Pedophiles, criminals, and other wolves looking to prey upon innocents must not be given free reign among the flock. Single women and children are especially vulnerable; brothers and sisters in the Lord must have the boldness and courage to speak directly about such matters to rescue those being led to the slaughter. Churches must be bold enough to deal with this issue.

I received a real healing at a *Freedom in Christ* seminar led by Neil Anderson when he directly addressed those issues. He wanted, at one point, to establish an alliance with a women's shelter, but they wanted nothing to do with him as a Christian Pastor. Why? Because so many of the women who go to their shelters are Christian women and the church refused to bring abusive husbands to accountability or report them to authorities. Often the women were simply told to return home and try harder to be good, submissive wives. Neil Anderson stood in front of thousands of women and asked our forgiveness for all the ways in which men have abused or mistreated us. The Spirit of God moved in that man's humility and a great emotional healing took place, not only in my heart, but I know in the hearts of many women that day.

It is my hope and prayer that this portion of my testimony will help to bring healing and restoration to the hearts of men and women and that God would be glorified in all our relationships. God is a merciful God and longs to bring restoration in people's lives. After walking through the valley of the shadow of death, the Good Shepherd began to lead me beside quieter waters as He began the process of restoring my soul (Psalm 23).

CHAPTER SEVEN

Two Are Better Than One

"Two are better than one, because they have a good return for their work."

Eccelesiastes 4:9 (NIV)

After a wrenching separation and divorce, the Holy Spirit directed my steps back to my hometown and to a Messianic Congregation. There I met a godly man from Poland. It was a divine appointment. The first time I noticed him, he had a letter clutched tightly in his hand. He seemed quite excited about it and was trying to show it to the pastor at the mid-week Bible study. I overheard it was from a woman in Poland who wanted to marry him and move to Israel. After the study, as I drove home, I felt led to intercede for this man and so I prayed, "Dear God, You can see that this man needs a wife and is ready to be married. If this woman in the letter is the right one for him, then let it come to pass according to your will, but if this is not from you, then please bring just the right godly woman into his life to be his wife. Amen." Little did I know I was praying myself right into that job position!

The next time we had opportunity to meet, besides the *Shabbat* service, was at a *Purim* (Feast of Lots) play that I had written and was directing. This is a drama of the book of Esther that Jewish people often perform and celebrate each year. All parts were filled except one – that of the Eunuch. Fortunately for me, Eunuch was one word that was not yet in Radek's English vocabulary, and so he eagerly agreed to play the part. Radek always said, "Whatever you do, don't tell the part about *Purim* and the Eunuch!" How can I leave out the best part of the story?

We had a lot of fun doing the play together, and when a Jewish singles party came up, I suggested to him and another single that we go together. He agreed at first, but later called to cancel, feeling that he, as a simple taxi driver, an immigrant from Poland, was not in a class eligible to socialize with those people, most of whom were university graduates. It was then that I realized I really did have feelings for him and that if he was not going, then neither was I. That was a shock. I also had no idea that he was even remotely interested in me, since I was quite a bit older. Actually, he confessed that when he first met me and saw that I had three children, he assumed I was married and was envious of my non-existent husband. We ended up going to the party together with another friend. As I mingled with the other guests, I noticed him sitting in complete silence as several women perched themselves around him. "It's time for a rescue," I thought, and so I walked over to save him embarrassment and add some conversation to the group. He, I am sure, would give you an entirely different version of the scenario!

After we dropped off our friend, Radek then drove me home and on the way, shared his testimony. I felt moved with compassion to hear of how his decision for the Lord caused him to lose his wife and daughter as well as all his material possessions in the divorce. Being Catholic, his wife would not tolerate Radek's newfound zeal for the Lord and His Word. The Lord challenged Radekwith a question, "Would you be willing to give up everything for My sake?" Radek knew that his faith might cost him all he had, but he answered, "Yes." So the day came when his wife threw him, and his Bible, out of the house and changed the locks.

Radek grew up in a poverty-stricken, Catholic home in communist Poland, but through a series of near-fatal car accidents, the Lord finally got his attention. He was born again, baptized, and began attending a Polish Pentecostal Church. He also discovered a burning love within himself for Israel and the Jewish people, and received a strong prophetic word that he would go to minister among the lost sheep of the house of Israel.

Radek made himself available to help me in whatever way possible with the ministry – he was usually seen *schlepping*[1] box loads of heavy books. He studied Hebrew with me and was by far my best student. I think he had a crush on the teacher! We never dated; we were having too much fun doing the ministry together. Radek's idea of a date, was to take my run-down, on-its-last-legs, van to the car wash and bring it back sparkling clean. To me, as a single Mom, this was more appreciated than a movie or dinner.

Yes, I will admit that my heart leaped a bit and the earth did shake a touch at the sight of that handsome man; but, I was determined to keep the relationship platonic. It is not easy to trust again, and so I kept testing and testing, as only a woman can. I tested his character – the sincerity of his commitment to the Lord, his honesty, and his patience. Although I tried to trip him up or find some secret, hidden fault or sin, his life seemed to be solidly founded upon The Rock. It takes a special kind of love to relate to a wounded woman. I am convinced that only a man filled with the Spirit of God can demonstrate the kind of selfless, sacrificial love that the Messiah revealed to us (Ephesians 5:25-28). It takes a

---

1 Schlepping - Yiddish expression for carrying or lugging something; usually meaning something heavy or burdensome.

great deal of giving, over a long period of time, without receiving much of anything in return.

I was very cautious about our relationship, because I had learned through experience, and also, I had seen other single believers struggle and fall. Relationships seem to be one of the primary sand traps used by the enemy to bring people down. I see so many women still looking to man as their prince and rescuer while confessing the Lord as their Savior. Indeed, I had made the same mistake in the past and suffered terrible consequences as a result. I did not want to make the same mistake again – looking to man for my help. I wanted to look always to God, who created the Heavens and the Earth from where my help comes. I did not want to do anything that was not in the perfect will of God. So I resisted, and resisted, and resisted, while David continued to demonstrate the fruits of the spirit – love, joy, peace, patience, kindness, goodness, faithfulness, gentleness and self-control. He wanted to marry me. I had my doubts as to whether re-marriage was even a Biblical option for me after divorce.

The issue of whether I say, "I do" or "I don't" started to steal my peace, and so I prayed earnestly to the Lord to show me His will in the matter once and for all. We were scheduled to travel to a nearby city the next day for a presentation on the feast of *Chanukah*. I had all the books and materials I would need packed the night before, so as not to forget anything. One box, containing the special things I would need for the presentation, was wrapped in bright *Chanukah* wrapping paper and set aside. Radek loaded the van and then drove my van on the icy highway. Along the way, he said that he had a sense the Lord had some kind of special blessing for us that day, although he was not sure what it was about. I was intrigued. When we arrived at the church and Radek unloaded all the boxes, I looked for the special *Chanukah* box, but it was nowhere to be found! It had been left behind. I began to panic, but then gave it all to the Lord and confessed my need of His grace. Someone found a small *Chanukiah* (candle holder) for the occasion and the presentation went very well.

Afterwards, we were invited for lunch to a friend's home, and a vivacious, outgoing woman from the church joined us. During the lunch, she began to share about her painful experience as a woman in an abusive marriage and her difficulty in re-gaining trust. She shared about meeting her current husband, and how she tested his character, and his patience with her lack of response. We laughed as she told us that she broke off the relationship at least twenty five times, telling him she never wanted to see him again. Surely, I had not broken off our relationship as many times as she had – but probably very nearly. She gave testimony that after many years of marriage, her husband continued to demonstrate the kind of love that heals which can only originate in and flow from the heart of God.

Because we wanted to be married in time for Radek to accompany me to speak at the International Ministries to Israel's annual dinner banquet and to appear on a Christian television programme, we set the date for the day our flight was to leave. The leader of the ministry, hearing that this would be our honeymoon generously provided us with a lovely room in a hotel. We planned to have a very small and private ceremony in my home.

The week prior to the set wedding date, Radekattended a Messianic *yeshiva* – a week of intensive study with Messianic rabbis – in another city. I think he knew, and certainly the Lord knew, that I needed this time alone in order to gather courage to take this bold leap of faith. Even though the Lord had revealed His will to me, I still entertained doubts and fears. The Lord had done a wonderful healing in my mind, body, and spirit, but I knew that some memories lingered and some of the pain of abandonment remained unhealed. I did not know if I could love or trust again to the depth that would be required of me in marriage. One night, driving in the car, I suddenly felt the presence of the Lord and, even though I did not hear an audible voice, I heard with my spirit His gentle and reassuring voice. "Hannah, don't be afraid of marrying this man." He said, "I will heal you and show you My love through him." I wept in relief, and on our wedding day, walked down the stairs with confidence that God's blessing was upon this union. The Lord has proved His promise true.

I wondered if Radek would change after marriage. He teased me by asking if I was still waiting for him to change into the kind of man who watches sports obsessively on television, belches, and then calls to his wife for another beer!

Of course, time, as well as the unique challenges of a blended family, working together in ministry, and living under the constant threat of terrorism from suicide bombers, persecution from Orthodox Jews, and the general stress of life in Israel, has revealed the darker side of each of our personalities and characters. To be honest, there were times in Israel when I looked at my husband and asked myself, "Is this the man I married?" At times, the enemy has tried to come and steal our testimony through strife, division, and unforgiveness. No man is perfect. No woman is perfect either, which is why we desperately need the Holy Spirit and the grace of God to survive.

There have been times when I have wondered if I did the right thing in starting all over again at forty with a new marriage and having babies. I have found that energy levels are just not the same to endure those sleepless nights after forty as they were at twenty. In the face of judgement and criticism from some fellow Christians, I have wrestled with the issue of divorce and re-marriage in light of the words of *Yeshua*. "And I say to you, whoever divorces his wife, except for sexual immorality, and marries another, commits adultery; and whoever marries her who is divorced commits adultery." (Matthew 19:9) In all this, I can only lift my voice to heaven and say, "Have mercy upon me, O Lord, a sinner." I have found that even if we have gotten ourselves into a mess, the same God who would stoop to fish me out of a toilet in a hotel, who would lower himself to descend from heaven to die on the cross as a criminal, having committed no crime, but to sacrifice his life for my sins, is the same One who will help us with any mess we foolish children of His have got ourselves into - If we cry out for His mercy and grace.

Therefore, I am not advocating re-marriage after divorce, but to fervently seek the Holy Spirit on this issue. Many times we think that marriage is going to solve our problems only to find that we have simply traded in the problems we had as a single person for more complicated problems in marriage. One would be well advised to heed the apostle Paul's words when he said that it is easier to serve the Lord without the distractions of husband or wife and children, and that, in his opinion, a woman would be happier to remain single (1Corinthians 7:32-35, 40). On the other hand, a marriage partner and children can bring balance and through the continual sacrifice they demand, counteract our innate tendency towards selfishness. Single mothers with children need to be especially careful of the person they are marrying, keeping in mind that this person will not only become her husband but her children's father.

No, my husband is not my Savior, not my Messiah, not perfect. My God stands alone and exalted in that position; and if I ever forget, the Lord has ways of reminding me. There are times when even the most wonderful spouse will fail to meet our needs, and that is when we lift our eyes up to the mountains, to where our help comes. For our help comes from the Lord, maker of heaven and earth. People can be a blessing; but God is the source of every good thing. He is our provider, our healer, and our peace. We are to seek Him first, and all the things we need will be added unto us. There is a big difference between seeking God first, and seeking a mate first. I believe this is a major challenge for single believers. We can trust God in the area of our most intimate relationships.

Hannah's maternal grandparents, Esther & Jacob, from Poland

Hannah's Mom and three sisters on the farm in Peace River country

**Hannah's Mom & Dad
married under the chuppah, 1955**

**Hannah (One Year Old) with her big sister
December 1959**

Baby Hannah

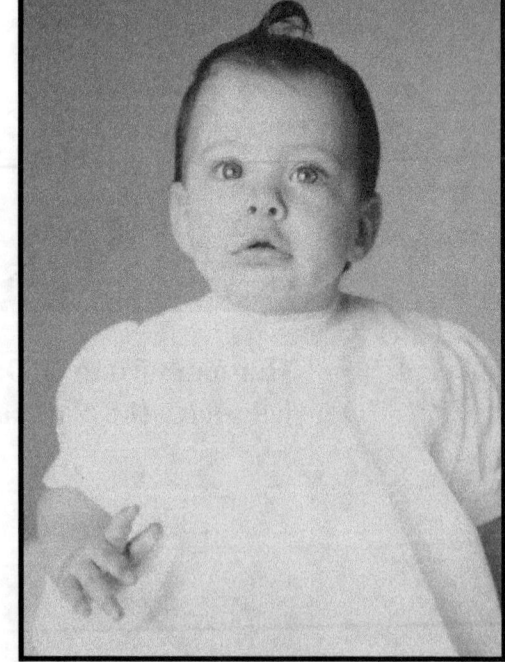

Family photo (Hannah at right)

Hannah (age 12) dancing at her *Bat Mitvah* party with her little brother Marc

Hannah in her Girl Guides Brownie uniform

Hannah as a teenager

Family photo c.1973

Hannah (left) with her cousin posing with Santa

Hannah as a single mom with Clayton & Courtney

Hannah petting a camel in Israel 1985

Hannah with Israeli soldiers

Hannah with her son Clayton at her graduation from University of Alberta Faculty of Education 1991

Hannah far (left) in a traditional Kimono with a group of Japanese students

Hannah gives birth at home to a healthy baby boy June 24th, 1993

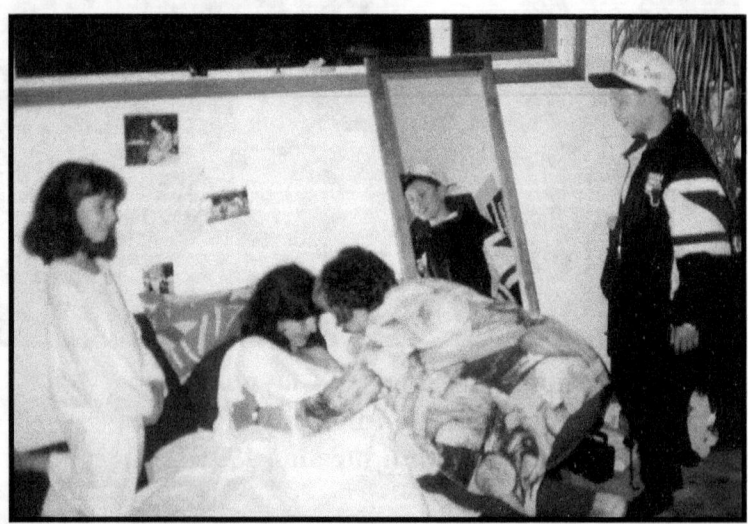

Two Are Better Than One

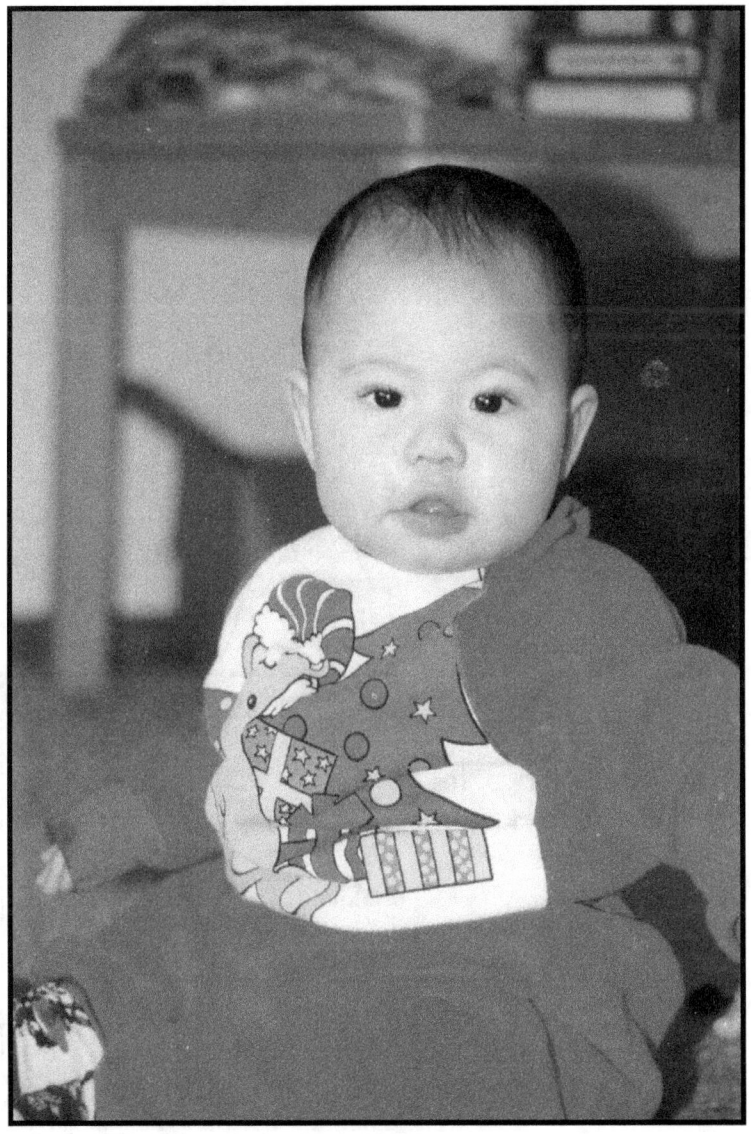

Timothy six months old on cover of Pregnancy Care Center Christmas Card Dec 1993

Timothy playing in the sand box

Timothy, age two, in his New York suit

Hannah and Radek married under the Tallit (Prayer Shawl)

**Nesher family
Radek, Hannah, Timothy, Liat and
Aviad 2003**

Timothy in Israel dressed as an IDF soldier for Purim

Timothy at the Kotel (Western Wall in Jerusalem)

Timothy blowing the shofar at the Kotel, 2003

Timothy blowing the shofar in Israel in 2013, 10 years later

Timothy graduating from high school in Jerusalem

Tim studying engineering at the Technion

Timothy in Jerusalem

Timothy & Victoria's wedding in Israel

Kasumi & Hideo at Timothy and Victoria's wedding

Hannah, Liat & Avi in Israel, 2015

CHAPTER EIGHT

Confession And Repentance

Healing may be found through *Yeshua's* blood, which sealed a new covenant of forgiveness and restoration. The various self-help groups available, as well-meaning as they may be, cannot ultimately help us. Abortion is a grave sin. This fact must be faced and acknowledged, not denied. We do not help people by telling them to simply forget about it and go on with your life. We must squarely face our sins, confess them and repent. Only then may we find healing and forgiveness.

> **If we confess our sins, he is faithful and just and will forgive us our sins and purify us from all unrighteousness.**
>
> 1 John 1:9 (NIV)

I remember going for a weekend retreat with the children while pregnant with Timothy. Everywhere I went, I looked for sympathy and pity as an abandoned woman. Indeed, I felt very sorry for myself, but a Christian woman helped me see my situation with a clearer perspective. The hostel in the mountains that I visited was owned by Christians. When I shared my tale of woe with the wife, instead of receiving the usual *tsk, tsk* of sympathy and consolation, she confronted me with the fact that it was my sin that placed me in this predicament. Sex apart from a marriage covenant is considered a sin in the Bible and called fornication. Although common in our modern society and culture, God's view remains unchanged by our changing standards of morality. An intimate sexual relationship is to be reserved for a man and woman joined together in a lifetime covenant of marriage, not by a temporary physical attraction. So although I felt shocked and hurt by this woman's seeming lack of compassion, this was exactly the jolt I needed to see that it was my own sin that had messed up my life. The Bible says a man perverts his ways and then his heart rages against God (Proverbs 19:3). I needed to repent, clean up my act, and commit myself to holiness and purity.

Whatever our sin, if we will get out of denial, face it, confess it, and call upon the grace of God to forgive it, we will not only be forgiven, but also be cleansed of all unrighteousness. We can experience freedom from the bondage of sin and a new start in life. God is gracious and merciful, rich in lovingkindness and slow to anger, always waiting with open arms for prodigal children to come to their senses and run home to *Abba* (Father).

Child Sacrifice Defiles the Land

The abortion issue today may be compared with the ancient crime of child-sacrifice, practiced by the Israelites in Biblical times. The Lord directed Joshua to drive the pagan nations out of the land of ancient Israel because of their sins and wickedness. The children of Jacob (Israel) were meant to become God's model nation, a separate, holy people, a light to the other nations. He warned them not to imitate the ways of the pagan nations, but Israel did not listen, and thus provoked God's fury. The worst and most detestable sin that Israel committed was that of child sacrifice.

> **They even sacrificed their sons And their daughters to demons, And shed innocent blood, The blood of their sons and daughters, Whom they sacrificed to the idols of Canaan; and the land was polluted with blood.**
> Psalm 106:37-38 (HEB)

The shedding of innocent blood defiles and pollutes the land and God warned the people of Israel against it (Numbers 35:33). Today, since the innocent blood of so many babies is shed through abortion in the midst of our own nations, the guilt of bloodshed remains upon us and the land is defiled in God's sight. The Almighty says,

> **...You must purge from Israel the guilt of shedding innocent blood, so that it may go well with you.**
> Deuteronomy 19:13 (NIV)

I believe the same holds true for all the nations that are allowing the sacrificing of their sons and daughters to proceed unhampered by cries of protest. Most people justifiably lament the horror of the Holocaust, the ruthless and deliberate extermination of over six million Jewish people, and yet a holocaust just as deadly is happening in our midst today and we remain silent. Abortions are increasing in Israel as new immigrants arrive in whose backgrounds eight to ten abortions are not uncommon. The number of abortions performed upon Jewish lives is of such proportion that it may be compared to another holocaust. It may be more sophisticated, but it is the same spirit of death, violence, and selfishness in operation today to steal, murder, and destroy.

Approximately one hundred and fifty abortions are performed in Israel each day. Women in the army may receive two free abortions during their term of service. One speaker at an Israeli Pro Life Conference graphically brought this point across. He held up a Hebrew newspaper and noted the headline, *One Israeli*

Soldier Killed Today By Palestinian Terrorist. He began searching through the rest of the paper for any column or article stating that 150 Israeli children were killed today with the consent of their parents, doctors, and the Israeli government. Of course, no such article may be found.

All of us have a part to play in this issue. God held the Israelites responsible for sitting back passively and allowing their brethren to cause their children to pass through the fire to Molech. The sin of omission may be just as grave as that of commission.

> **"...Any Israelite or any alien living in Israel who gives any of his children to Molech must be put to death. The people of the community are to stone him...If the people of the community close their eyes...I will set my face against that man and his family and will cut off from their people both him and all who follow him in prostituting themselves to Molech."**
>
> Leviticus 20:1-4 (NIV)

We must speak up for those who have no voices and defend those who are not able to defend themselves.

> **Open your mouth for the speechless, In the cause of all who are appointed to die.**
>
> Proverbs 31:8 (HEB)

What are we doing to help rescue the unborn from slaughter?

> **Rescue those being led away to death; hold back those staggering toward slaughter. If you say, "But we knew nothing about this," does not he who weighs the heart perceive it? Does not he who guards your life know it?...**
>
> Proverbs 24:11-12 (NIV)

Surely the voice of all these infants' blood cries out to God from the ground, as did Abel's (Genesis 4:10). Because of the shedding of this innocent blood, we would be under a curse, but for *Yeshua*, the Mediator of the new covenant, whose blood speaks louder than the blood of Abel.

> **...Jesus the Mediator of the new covenant, and to the blood of sprinkling that speaks better things than that of Abel."**
>
> Hebrews 12:24 (HEB)

Facing the issue of abortion means confronting the same spiritual forces of darkness that demanded child sacrifice in ancient times. Today, the abortion rate among believers is unfortunately comparable to non-believers. The people of God may not be sacrificing to Molech today, but they are, nonetheless, sacrificing their children to gods of sexual immorality, materialism, convenience, and reputation. These things are taking higher priority than the Word of God which says, Thou shalt not murder, and declares anyone who does this is detestable to the Lord (Deuteronomy 18:10-12). Thank God for the blood of *Yeshua* that cleanses us from our sins. It washes us white as snow. Our sins are cast into the sea as far as the East is from the West!

Taking Back the Land

In Israel, during the Feast of Tabernacles, my son-in-law led a praise and worship music concert in the same valley where the Israelites used to offer up their children as sacrifices to Molech. As I watched the children gleefully running barefoot over the same ground where the Israelites once shed the blood of their children, a weeping overcame me. My tears expressed the gratitude of my soul to see these precious children alive, laughing, tumbling, singing, dancing – praising the Lord our God in this valley which had once been drenched with the blood of Israel's children. I also shed tears of sorrow and grief, for my own unborn children, whom I had sacrificed.

Under the law, I deserved to be stoned. The punishment for my sin was death. However, just as the woman who committed adultery was brought to *Yeshua* and found mercy in His presence, so may we find mercy through Him for all the sins we have ever committed. Most women who choose abortion, as I did in the past, really do not know any better and are not conscious of the sin they are committing. Rather than judging in a self-righteous manner, we need to show mercy and say, Father, forgive them, for they know not what they are doing. We must pray for women to choose life, not only for their unborn children but also for their own eternal souls through faith in *Yeshua* the Messiah.

Beauty Instead of Ashes

Yeshua is the only answer and our only hope. In sharing my testimony, I invariably find people in the group who have been affected by the issue of abortion; women who, when faced with the choice of life or death for their unborn child chose death, men who encouraged or even pressured an abortion decision, parents who supported their child in their decision to abort, and some who still grieve over the loss of their child or grandchild because it occurred against their will. *Yeshua* came in part,

> **"...to heal the broken-hearted, To proclaim liberty for the captives, And the opening of the prison to those who are bound."**
>
> Isaiah 61:1 (HEB)

When the Jewish men read the *haftorah* (prophetic portion of scripture) in the synagogue one *Shabbat*, *Yeshua* rolled up the *Torah* scroll and said,

> "...Today this scripture is fulfilled in your hearing."
>
> Luke 4:21 (HEB)

These promises are available today through the Messiah for any who will receive them. He offers a wonderful exchange –

> ...a crown of beauty instead of ashes, the oil of gladness instead of mourning, and a garment of praise instead of a spirit of despair...
>
> Isaiah 61:3 (NIV)

The Mercy Seat

God has a plan and purpose for each child even before he or she emerges from the womb, even before that child is conceived, just as He did for the prophet Jeremiah.

> "Before I formed you in the womb I knew you, before you were born I set you apart; I appointed you as a prophet to the nations."
>
> Jeremiah 1:5 (NIV)

King David knew that it was his heavenly Father who actually formed him in his mother's womb.

> For you created my inmost being; you knit me together in my mother's womb. I praise you because I am fearfully and wonderfully made...My

> frame was not hidden from you when I was made in the secret place. When I was woven together in the depths of the earth, your eyes saw my unformed body. All the days ordained for me were written in your book before one of them came to be.
>
> Psalm 139:13-16 (NIV)

The womb, called the *rechem* in Hebrew, comes from the same root as the Hebrew word for mercy. This seat of mercy should be a safe, secure haven for the growing infant, where it receives warmth, nourishment, and protection; and yet, it is now the most dangerous place in the world for a baby to live. In both Hebrew and Greek, the Bible makes no distinction linguistically between the child within or outside of the womb. We must come to grips with the fact that babies within their mothers' wombs are truly human beings.

God looks upon the unformed bodies of these tiny infants in the womb. He sees when they are murdered. He has said,

> **"You shall not murder."**
>
> Exodus 20:13 (NIV)

These precious lives are not random blobs of fetal tissue, as some like to claim. God has a book and writes in it His plans for each of these children even before they are born. How many pages of His wonderful plans lie perpetually unfulfilled because the ones written about were never given the opportunity to live out their God-ordained lives? Life is holy to God and it is not ours to take. Ours is a culture that often considers children liabilities rather than blessings. Large families are sometimes frowned upon; people stare and wonder what must be wrong with the woman who chooses to bear many children. The Bible says that children are our reward (in Hebrew the word indicates they are our salary) and,

> **Happy is the man who has his quiver full of them...**
>
> Psalm 127:5 (HEB)

In many parts of the world, fertility is seen as a great blessing from God. But if we perceive children as an annoyance, nuisance, or inconveniene to our busy lifestyles or obstacles preventing our goals, then surely we will want to at least prevent their conception. Satan always seeks to kill the seed. If we cooperate with his evil plans, then we place ourselves under his cover of darkness. God wants us to choose life, not death for our children.

Yeshua is the Way

As you know, I do not write this from a high and mighty self-righteousness and judgment towards those who have suffered through abortion. I am, as the apostle Paul said, chief sinner among the sinners.

> **...Christ Jesus came into the world to save sinners – of whom I am the worst. But for that very reason I was shown mercy so that in me, the worst of sinners, Christ Jesus might display his unlimited patience as an example of those who would believe on him and receive eternal life.**
>
> 1 Timothy 1:15-16 (NIV)

I offer my life story as an example of someone who has fallen very, very low, and found that there is no place deep enough that God's everlasting arms of mercy will not reach down to scoop us out of the miry clay and set our feet on the solid rock.

> **Where can I go from Your Spirit? Or where can I flee from Your presence? If I ascend into heaven, You are there; If I make my bed in hell, behold, You are there. If I take the wings of the morning, And dwell in the uttermost parts of the sea...**
>
> Psalm 139:7-9 (HEB)

Yeshua stooped so low as to endure a cruel and humiliating death as a criminal, even though completely innocent, in order that we can walk with our heads lifted up. I used to feel that I could never be real with people; that if they accepted me it was only because they did not know the real me – the one who had murdered her own children. I felt almost as if there was an invisible scarlet mark on my forehead forever identifying me as such. I walked with my head held low, but He is the glory and the lifter of our heads. I obviously have not written about my own personal sins and failings in order to bring glory to myself, but rather that some may be set free, and turn back to the living God, just as David prayed after confronted with his sin with Batsheva.

> **Create in me a pure heart, O God, and renew a steadfast spirit within me...Restore to me the joy of your salvation and grant me a willing spirit, to sustain me. Then I will teach transgressors your ways, and sinners will turn back to you. Save me from bloodguilt, O God, the God who saves me, and my tongue will sing of your righteousness.**
>
> Psalm 51:10-14 (NIV)

If this issue of abortion speaks to your heart, or if the Holy Spirit has convicted of you of any sin – if you need to find divine forgiveness and healing – please pray this prayer and rest in the assurance of God's abundant grace and mercy towards us, for He knows that we are but dust. He loves each and every one of us so much, that while we were yet sinners, even those of us who sacrificed our own children, He, the Messiah died for us (Romans 5:8). *Yeshua* did not come for the righteous, but for the sinners, just as the doctor is not for the healthy, but for the sick. Even this day, I told my husband that I sometimes hesitate sharing about the Lord because of the areas of my life that are still under construction. In other words, some areas of my life and my character still need the transforming power of the Holy Spirit to change me into the image of the Almighty. But my husband reminded me that it is exactly for us, regular people who need Him desperately, that *Yeshua* came to earth to die on the cross and be resurrected. The Word of God says,

> **... for all have sinned and fall short of the glory of God.**
>
> Romans 3:23 (NIV)

and,

> **If we claim we have not sinned, we make him out to be a liar and his word has no place in our lives.**
>
> 1 John 1:10 (NIV)

He did not come for perfect people – He came for sinners like each of us.

"Well, what if I am Jewish?" you may ask. *Yeshua* came from the tribe of Judah, born a son to a Jewish virgin maiden (Isaiah 7:14, 9:6). The New Testament identifies the mother of this son, who would one day inherit the throne of his father David, as a Jewish maiden named *Miryam* (Mary) (Luke 1:30-33). He was circumcised on the eighth day (Luke 1:59) according to the Law of Moses. He lived a sinless life according to all the principles of the *Torah*. All his disciples and most of his first followers were also Jewish. Almost all the writers of the New Testament were Jewish too. To say that we cannot believe in or follow a Jewish Messiah because we are Jewish is ridiculous! It is only an emotional, irrational belief.

"Well, then, what if I am a Gentile?" Salvation came to the world through the Jewish people. He is the Lion of the tribe of Judah and will return as such to judge the earth. But that does not mean He came exclusively for the Jewish people. This would have been too small or insignificant a mission for the Messiah, the prophet Isaiah told us. Jesus is also a Light for the Gentiles. He came to bring salvation – the meaning of his Hebrew name, *Yeshua* – to the ends of the earth; to every tongue and tribe of people.

> **"...It is too small a thing for you to be my servant to restore the tribes of Jacob and bring back those of Israel I have kept. I will also make you a light for the Gentiles, that you may bring my salvation to the ends of the earth."**
> Isaiah 49:6 (NIV)

It makes no difference whatsoever whether we are Jew or Gentile, male or female. There is only one way to the Father and the Messiah is the only way.

> **"I am the way and the truth and the life. No one comes to the Father except through me."**
> John 14:6 (NIV)

Come now, to the Father, the God of Abraham, Isaac, and Jacob, through the forgiveness found in the sacrifice of *Yeshua*, the Messiah. You can pray this prayer or something spontaneous out of your own heart:

Confession and Repentance

God of Abraham, Isaac & Jacob (Israel), You have forbidden us to pray to anyone but You and so I now pray to You and to You alone. You know me. You knit me together in my mother's womb and wrote a plan for my life in Your book even before I was born; and yet, I have wandered away from you like a sheep wanders away from its shepherd and becomes lost. Thank you for not giving up until You found me, and brought me back to lie down in green pastures. Please be my Good Shepherd once again and lead me beside quiet waters and restore my soul. Please forgive me for my sins, (even for the sin of sacrificing my child(ren) through abortion or _____).

Thank you for providing atonement for all of my sins, both secret and known, through the punishment You laid upon Yeshua, Your Son. Please cleanse me from all sin and all unrighteousness with His precious blood.

I know that You can turn whatever was meant for evil into something used for Your good purposes. I know You have a wonderful plan and purpose for my life. Please help me, Adonai (Lord), to walk now in the ways You have commanded Your children, in a way that pleases You. Circumcise my heart that I may love you with all my heart and soul and strength and love my neighbour as myself. Please create in me a new heart and renew a new spirit within me according to the New Covenant, sealed in the blood of Yeshua.

Thank you for welcoming me home and casting my sins into the depths of the sea that they may never again be remembered by You, nor held against me in any way. Please renew my mind, cleanse my conscience, my body, soul, and spirit of all defilement by the blood of Yeshua and the power of the Holy Spirit. Restore to me my purity, and help me by Your grace, to walk in holiness. I will always remember Your kindness towards me and I will call upon You for as long as I shall live. I will share about Your goodness and mercy with others as You lead and guide me. Amen

Note: If you prayed this prayer, I would love to hear from you. Please contact me at the address at the beginning of this book. This prayer is not a formula that gets you into heaven, but the first step to a new life with God. *Yeshua* is not a 'get out of hell free' card; but, He is our Savior, Redeemer, Deliverer, and Friend and so much more. Four more events are necessary to continue growing in the Lord:

1) *Mikvah* (ritual water immersion)
2) Being filled with the Holy Spirit
3) Regular study of the Word of God and prayer; praise and worship
4) Becoming part of the flock – planted in a Bible-based, spirit-filled Congregation under the care of a leader who is a true undershepherd of *Yeshua*. Lone sheep easily stray and are prime targets for wolves. Keep meeting with other Believers.

A Special Note to PAS Women

For those women suffering from the aftermath of the trauma of abortion, called Post Abortion Syndrome (PAS), my heart goes out to you. Sometimes we are so numb that we live in denial of the pain, but it shows up in other ways, some of which may include self-destructive tendencies, promiscuity, uncontrolled anger, recurring problems in relationships, depression, suicidal inclinations, undefined guilt, difficulty bonding with other children, and obsession with pregnancy. If these symptoms plague your life, it may be that your past continues to torment you because of an abortion or perhaps multiple abortions.

Not everyone, even those who love you, may know how to help. You may need additional counseling from caring, compassionate professionals, trained in guiding women through the process of healing and forgiveness. For me, I received closure to my grief through a post-abortion small group Bible study organized and facilitated by a counselor with the local Pregnancy Care Centre. I believe that most Crisis Pregnancy Centres offer a similar study or program of counseling. We met together each week, shared our stories, and studied the Word of God. We cried together, prayed together and even occasionally found that we could laugh together. In the beginning, I did not connect with my guilt or pain over my abortions; I did not fully understand the gravity of my sin. Once the realization hit, however, I needed those precious women to hold me up and assure me of the unconditional love that God still had for me through *Yeshua*. At the end of our study, we held a group memorial for all of our unborn babies that had perished through abortion. Some women named them; some wrote poems or said a few words to their child; some asked their forgiveness. Our counselor gave each of us a rose to hold, representing the flowers we would lay on the tiny graves, had they existed. It was a sober moment for us all. Then a woman sat at the piano and began to sing with the most beautiful voice the song, which will always remind me, even in my darkest hours, of why I live and how I find the courage to face each day of my life.

> *Because He lives I can face tomorrow*
> *Because He lives All fear is gone*
> *Because I know He holds the future*
> *Then life is worth the living*
> *Just because He lives.*

I cannot, with absolute truth, testify that I no longer suffer any consequences from my past experiences with abortion. There are times when, as I gaze with absolute wonder at the miracle of my newest baby and see the joy he brings to my life, I still break down and weep at the knowledge of the babies I casually discarded as if simply another piece of trash. My comfort is in knowing that each one of my babies that never saw the light of day on this earth is now in heaven with *Yeshua. My hope is that* one day I will hold them in my arms.

Just recently, I had the privilege of listening to another woman give her testimony of healing and transformation from Post Abortion Syndrome. It amazed me how deeply her testimony touched me and how her experience still evoked such intense emotions in all of us, even after so many years. It is my hope through revealing our wounds and scars that you, my beloved sister, will find healing, just as we are healed by *Yeshua's* wounds. Please don't live in denial or just suffer in silence. Reach out for the help that is there for you – and remember – I'll be praying for you.

> **…Weeping may endure for a night, But joy comes in the morning. You have turned for me my mourning into dancing; You have put off my sackcloth and clothed me with gladness, To the end that my glory may sing praise to You and not be silent. O LORD my God, I will give thanks to You forever.**
>
> Psalm 30:5, 11 (HEB)

Conclusion – Dayeinu

Even though the *Jewish Roots* ministry in Canada grew and flourished, my husband and I could no longer ignore the call to Israel. The amazing account of God's guidance through the wilderness and into the Promised Land is material for another book. So we now come full circle – from the depths of sin and despair to the heights of joy and salvation. At each Passover Seder, we sing a song called *Dayeinu*, which is roughly translated *it is enough*:

> "If the Lord had only delivered us from Egypt and not parted the Red Sea – *Dayeinu*.
>
> If the Lord had parted the Red Sea, and not given us manna in the wilderness – *Dayeinu*.
> If the Lord had given us manna in the wilderness, but had not given us the Sabbath – *Dayeinu*.
>
> If the Lord had given us the Sabbath and not given us the *Torah* at Mt. Sinai – *Dayeinu*…"

On and on the song continues in ever-increasing realization of all that the Lord has done for us as a nation. We are, at the Passover, to consider ourselves as personally delivered from bondage into freedom. In reviewing all that the Lord has done for me, I also think, *Dayeinu*! He has saved my soul and that of my children, freely giving us what we did not deserve – a place with Him eternally in heaven, the restored Garden of Eden. He saved the life of my precious son, Timothy (named Shmuel in Hebrew which means Samuel), from abortion, without whom my existence now would be inconceivable and has blessed me with other beautiful children, as well as grandchildren! He has given me a wonderful husband who loves us and serves the Lord with all his heart. And so, although I say a heartfelt *Dayeinu* to the Lord for all He has done in my life and all He has given to me by His grace, I continue to look forward to the new things He has in store for the future.

Timothy's biological father once said to me, "You know my heart," but only God truly knows our hearts. He will never leave nor forsake us.

Trust God. Put your hope in Him. Choose Life!

> **This day I call heaven and earth as witnesses against you that I have set before you life and death, blessings and curses. Now choose life, so that you and your children may live...**
>
> Deuteronomy. 30:19 (NIV)

I ask God to bless you and keep you and to make His face shine upon you and to give you *shalom* (peace). Surely He has wonderful plans for us all – for good and not for evil, to give us a hope and a future. Seek God with all your heart, for He has promised that those who seek Him will find Him (Jeremiah 29:11-13). I pray that this book has spoken to your heart in a special way that can only come from the Spirit of God.

> **"The LORD יהוה bless you and keep you;**
> **The LORD יהוה make His face shine upon you,**
> **And be gracious to you;**
> **The LORD יהוה lift up His countenance upon you,**
> **And give you peace."**
>
> Numbers 6: 24-26 (HEB)

> **"Oh, give thanks to the LORD, for He is good! For His mercy endures forever."**
>
> Ps 136:1 (HEB)

Postscript

Since the writing of this book, so many years have passed; and so much has changed that it calls for a postscript. It didn't seem to me quite appropriate to just add a *'P.S. I'm divorced again, and raising two more children as a single Mom.'* If you have read this far, then surely you deserve more of an explanation that this simplistic statement; because we all know that life is rarely simple – or easy.

When asked, in Hebrew, for an answer that requires a lengthy explanation, we often reply, *"Oye, zeh sipur aroch."* This means literally, 'It's a long story!' Usually the Israeli will simply nod their head in understanding. Life happens. Enough said...

I have struggled to know how to end this book in a way that still gives glory to God; in this I must trust the Ruach Hakodesh (Holy Spirit) to speak to your heart through these final words.

In every story there is always the good news and the bad news. The good news is that Timothy eventually had the opportunity to meet his biological father, Hiroshi, in Japan; and we were able to express forgiveness to each other. How did this come about? At a pro-life (Be'ad Chaim) conference in Israel, we met a precious Japanese Christian woman named Kasumi. She heard my testimony about Timothy and was so touched that she promised to one day bring him to Japan as a Bar Mitzvah gift.

Incredibly, Kasumi kept her promise and when Timothy turned thirteen, she sent us two tickets to Japan. We had such a wonderful time with Kasumi and her friends, meeting with Japanese Christians (who are a small minority in the nation of Japan), and ministering together around the country. The highlight of our visit, however, was that Kasumi had pre-arranged a meeting between Timothy's father (Hiroshi) and ourselves at a small café.

I felt so nervous that I was shaking, as it had been fourteen years since we had seen each other. Hiroshi was obviously nervous as well. Only Timothy seemed his usual, carefree, joyful self. The two of them sitting together looked like two peas in a pod; the resemblance between them was striking. We both wept as he asked for my forgiveness and I expressed my complete forgiveness towards him. I then shared that even though I forgave him; it was more important that he knows God's forgiveness in his heart through the Messiah Yeshua.

Although we have had very little contact with Timothy's father over the years, I feel that we had closure and am thankful for the opportunity I had to share Yeshua's love with him. Incredibly, we have stayed in touch with Kasumi all these years and when Timothy married his childhood sweetheart, Victoria, under the chuppah in Israel, Kasumi and her husband came to help us celebrate.

At the time of this writing (2016), Timothy is preparing to graduate from the Technion's International School of Engineering in Haifa, Israel. Look at what the Lord has done! I praise Him for His wonderful goodness and give Him all the glory and honor.

The story of our aliyah – how we immigrated to the Land of Israel – has been chronicled in the book, *Journey to Jerusalem*.

I don't propose to repeat myself here – the good, the bad or the ugly of that life-changing experience. Suffice to say it was quite the wild ride with hair-pin twists and turns.

The good news is that during the time of our marriage and years in Israel, I gave birth to two amazing children. At the time of this writing, they are both teenagers: Liat has reached the age of 'sweet sixteen' and Avi entered the world of double digits at thirteen. Both are officially 'sabras' (slang for native born Israelis) and are fluent in both Hebrew and English.

So how did a marriage that started off so wonderfully end in divorce? Like many divorced people, we probably can only shake our heads and say, "I honestly don't know." There is always the tendency to blame the other spouse; but in reality there are usually two valid sides to every story. I have no desire to go into the gory details but suffice to say I had biblical justification for divorce.

Attempting to adjust to life in a new (Middle Eastern) country with a completely different culture and language only several months into a new marriage and blended family probably didn't help. It is difficult enough to make aliyah with a solid foundation; let alone with one that was already shaky and badly cracked. Living in a country besieged by terrorism; and being evicted from such same country likely didn't help matters either.

Dysfunctional backgrounds, generation and individual sin, rebellion, trauma, baggage from the past – all these things seem to have a way of combining into one gigantic destructive force that defies all attempts to withstand the carnage. In the end, separation seemed the only answer to any kind of sane existence; and after several failed attempts to reconcile, the children and I moved back to Israel in December 2009 on our own.

Although David (he changed his name from Radek while in Canada) attempted to follow us into the country, he was arrested and deported due to a visa violation. The children and I stayed in Israel while he lived in Canada until we divorced in 2014. He is now remarried and in the process of rebuilding his life. We maintain a good relationship now – from a distance.

In conclusion, what can be said? Only that we are broken, imperfect vessels trying to do our best with living in this fallen world. Life outside of Eden can be painful; and as followers of Yeshua, we are not immune to being pricked by the thorns and broken by the trials. Yeshua did warn us that in this life we would have trouble, but we can still be joyful for He has overcome the world.

Our hope is not in this world – not in our relationships, our jobs, our money or our ministries. All these things may pass away – but there is yet that One who remains faithful, steadfast and true – and that is our God.

I began my relationship with my God by hearing the words, "He will never leave you or forsake you." This is still His promise to us – no matter what else has or is being shaken in our lives. We have a Rock upon which we can securely stand. We have a hope that is an anchor for our souls. We have a safe shelter from the storms of life under His wings. We have a faithful provider – a generous 'Abba' (Father) who will supply all of our needs in a way that no human being is able.

Sometimes life takes us in directions that we didn't expect; we had hoped for a different outcome; and yet we know that His plan for our lives is good – to give us a hope and a future. He is a refuge for us; and is very near to those who are broken-hearted.

PostScript

I had hoped to end my story with a perfect testimony that I am happily married to a wonderful man; but perhaps God has a different message. Maybe God wants us to remember that He is the One who is absolutely faithful. We can trust in Him – no matter what happens – because we are in Covenant with Him; and He will be there for us in sickness or in health, for richer or for poorer….and even beyond death He is there.

> **The Lord is my shepherd, I lack nothing.**
>
> **He makes me lie down in green pastures,**
> **He leads me beside quiet waters,**
> **He refreshes my soul.**
>
> **He guides me along the right paths for His name's sake.**
> **Even though I walk through the darkest valley**
> **I will fear no evil, for You are with me;**
> **your rod and your staff, they comfort me.**
> (Psalm 23:1-4)

In this world, there are many blessings and causes to rejoice; but there are also times when we walk through the Valley of Bacca (weeping). Even these valleys of weeping can, in the Lord's hands, become a place of blessing that brings living waters of refreshing to others who are weary and thirsty:

> **"When they walk through the Valley of Weeping, it will become a place of refreshing springs. The autumn rains will clothe it with blessings."**
> (Psalm 84:6)

In the end, all the cares and concerns of this world will one day pass away; and we will be in a glorious place where there will be no more tears or weeping or pain or sorrow; for He will wipe away every tear from our eyes and remove all shame.

> **"The Sovereign LORD will wipe away the tears from all faces; he will remove his people's disgrace from all the earth. The LORD has spoken."**
>
> (Isaiah 25:8)

> **"He will wipe away every tear from their eyes, and there will be no more death or mourning or crying or pain, for the former things have passed away."**
>
> (Revelation 21:4)

Until then, we must always remember to keep our eyes on Yeshua, the author and finisher or our faith; and He will keep our hearts and minds at peace as we continue to trust in Him. Keep looking up, for our redemption draws near. Be strong and of good courage, for the Lord our God is with us.

With much love (ahava) and shalom (peace)
Hannah

I had hoped to end my story with a perfect testimony that I am happily married to a wonderful man; but perhaps God has a different message. Maybe God wants us to remember that He is the One who is absolutely faithful. We can trust in Him – no matter what happens – because we are in Covenant with Him; and He will be there for us in sickness or in health, for richer or for poorer….and even beyond death He is there.

> **The Lord is my shepherd, I lack nothing.**
>
> **He makes me lie down in green pastures,**
> **He leads me beside quiet waters,**
> **He refreshes my soul.**
>
> **He guides me along the right paths for His name's sake.**
> **Even though I walk through the darkest valley**
> **I will fear no evil, for You are with me;**
> **your rod and your staff, they comfort me.**
> (Psalm 23:1-4)

In this world, there are many blessings and causes to rejoice; but there are also times when we walk through the Valley of Bacca (weeping). Even these valleys of weeping can, in the Lord's hands, become a place of blessing that brings living waters of refreshing to others who are weary and thirsty:

> **"When they walk through the Valley of Weeping, it will become a place of refreshing springs. The autumn rains will clothe it with blessings."**
> (Psalm 84:6)

In the end, all the cares and concerns of this world will one day pass away; and we will be in a glorious place where there will be no more tears or weeping or pain or sorrow; for He will wipe away every tear from our eyes and remove all shame.

> **"The Sovereign LORD will wipe away the tears from all faces; he will remove his people's disgrace from all the earth. The LORD has spoken."**
>
> (Isaiah 25:8)

> **"He will wipe away every tear from their eyes, and there will be no more death or mourning or crying or pain, for the former things have passed away."**
>
> (Revelation 21:4)

Until then, we must always remember to keep our eyes on Yeshua, the author and finisher or our faith; and He will keep our hearts and minds at peace as we continue to trust in Him. Keep looking up, for our redemption draws near. Be strong and of good courage, for the Lord our God is with us.

With much love (ahava) and shalom (peace)
Hannah

Isaiah 53

Surely he took up our infirmities and carried our sorrows, yet we considered him stricken by God, smitten by him, and afflicted. But he was pierced for our transgressions, he was crushed for our iniquities; the punishment that brought us peace was upon him, and by his wounds we are healed. We all, like sheep, have gone astray, each of us has turned to his own way; and the LORD has laid on him the iniquity of us all.

He was oppressed and afflicted, yet he did not open his mouth; he was led like a lamb to the slaughter, and as a sheep before her shearers is silent, so he did not open his mouth. By oppression and judgment he was taken away. And who can speak of his descendants? For he was cut off from the land of the living; for the transgression of my people he was stricken. He was assigned a grave with the wicked, and with the rich in his death, though he had done no violence, nor was any deceit in his mouth.

Yet it was the LORD'S will to crush him and cause him to suffer, and though the LORD makes his life a guilt offering, he will see his offspring and prolong his days, and the will of the LORD will prosper in his hand. After the suffering of his soul, he will see the light of life, and be satisfied; by his knowledge my righteous servant will justify many, and he will bear their iniquities. Therefore I will give him a portion among the great, and he will divide the spoils with the strong, because he poured out his life unto death, and was numbered with the transgressors. For he bore the sin of many, and made intercession for the transgressors.

Isaiah 53:4-12 (NIV)

To contact the Author write:

Hannah Nesher, Voice for Israel
Suite #313- 11007 Jasper Ave.
Edmonton, Alberta
T5K 0K6 Canada

www.voiceforisrael.net

Please include your testimony or help received from this book when you write.

Your prayer requests are welcome

Additional Teaching Materials by Hannah Nesher

DVDs

Shalom Morah I (Hebrew for Christians & Hebrew Names of God) 11 DVD set
Shalom Morah II (Hebrew for Christians & Wisdom in the Hebrew Alphabet) 10 DVD set
Exploring the Jewish Roots of the Christian Faith
Unity in the Messiah
Because He Lives
Messianic Jewish Wedding in Jerusalem
There is a God in Israel
Messianic Jewish Passover
Passover Lamb or Easter Ham?
Yom Hasho'ah (Where is Your Brother Jacob?)
Walking Through the Wilderness
Ruth: A Righteous Gentile
Esther's Last Call (Purim)
Blow the Shofar in Zion
Shalom Jerusalem (Yom Ha'atzma'ut)
Messiah in Chanukah

BOOKS

Journey to Jerusalem
Come Out of Her My People
Messiah Revealed in Purim
Messiah Revealed in the Sabbath
Messiah Revealed in the Passover
Messiah Revealed in the Fall Feasts
Messiah Revealed in Chanukah
Kashrut: The Biblical Dietary Laws
Messiah Revealed in Shavuot

If you enjoyed this book and would like to learn more, don't miss the companion DVD

BECAUSE HE LIVES

Because He Lives is Hannah's personal testimony of multiple abortions, resulting in depression, despair and divorce. Seeking answers led Hannah into New Age, the occult and idolatry. But what the enemy intended for evil in Hannah's life, God has turned for good, even for the saving of many lives. Halleluyah!

Filmed on location near Jerusalem, Israel, this annointed recording also contains a message from Timothy, Hannah's son, who was saved from abortion.

It is a message of life, hope, and forgiveness that must be seen! Powerful pro-life, pro-Jewish and pro-Yeshua message!

Hannah Nesher, Voice for Israel
Suite #313- 11007 Jasper Ave.
Edmonton, Alberta
T5K 0K6 Canada

www.voiceforisrael.net

www.ingramcontent.com/pod-product-compliance
Lightning Source LLC
LaVergne TN
LVHW051502070426
835507LV00022B/2882